The True You

You'd probably be the first one to admit that you're not perfect. After all, who knows better than you your many failures and weaknesses? In spite of your best efforts, you fall into the same old patterns of behavior, alternately creative and destructive, loving and violent—without even knowing why you do the things you do.

But you, yourself, are not the problem—the problem is that you are ignorant of your true nature. Who you picture yourself to be, and who you really are, are two very different people. And it is this fundamental misconception that causes your suffering and pain.

After you read this book, you'll know who and what you are. You'll discover how to live the principles of Kashmir Shaivism and experience personal power in a way you never thought possible. You'll come face to face with the "true you" and set your life on a permanent course of peace, happiness and well-being.

You stand on the threshold of a great spiritual adventure. From this point forward, your life can be totally different. Open this book and begin your inner journey to your true self.

D0301249

About the Author

J. R. Picken grew up in Washington state in a family of apple growers and cattle ranchers whose ancestors had settled in the Okanogon Valley long ago. While his younger sister expressed interest in carrying on the family business, John pursued a medical career, earning an M.D. and a Ph.D. from Case Western Reserve University in Cleveland by 1979.

It was there that Dr. Picken began seriously grappling with the questions that many of us face about the meaning of our lives and our place in the universe. In 1981, he traveled to Kashmir and met the great Shaivite master Swami Lakshmanjoo. He considers that meeting the beginning of his real education. Over the next several years, he returned to Kashmir several times to spend time with Lakshmanjoo and eventually began writing down his thoughts and experiences, now gathered in this book, which he hopes will inspire others with Lakshmanjoo's great wisdom.

Dr. Picken practices family medicine in Southern Florida, where he lives with his wife Cheryl and daughter Amanda.

To Write to the Author

If you wish to contact the author or would like more information about this book, please write to the author in care of Llewellyn Worldwide and we will forward your request. Both the author and publisher appreciate hearing from you and learning of your enjoyment of this book and how it has helped you. Llewellyn Worldwide cannot guarantee that every letter written to the author can be answered, but all will be forwarded. Please write to:

J. R. Picken, Ph.D., M.D.
℅ Llewellyn Worldwide
P.O. Box 64383, Dept. K522-3, St. Paul, MN 55164-0383, U.S.A.
Please enclose a self-addressed, stamped envelope or $1.00 to cover costs.
If outside the U.S.A., enclose an international postal reply coupon.

CREATOR, PROTECTOR, DESTROYER

Discover That You Are God

J. R. Picken, Ph.D., M.D.

1997
Llewellyn Publications
St. Paul, Minnesota 55164-0383, U.S.A.

FIRST EDITION
First Printing, 1997

Cover design: Tom Grewe
Interior photographs: J. R. Picken
Book design and layout: Jessica Thoreson
Editor: Rosemary Wallner
Project coordinators: Jessica Thoreson and Darwin Holmstrom

Library of Congress Cataloging-in-Publication Data
Picken, J. R. (John R.), 1947–
     Creator, protector, destroyer : discover that you are God / J. R.
     Picken. -- 1st ed.
       p.   cm.
     Includes bibliographical references and index.
     ISBN 1-56718-522-3 (pbk.)
     1. Kashmir Saivism--Doctrines. 2. Lakshman, Swami. I. Title.
     BL1281.1545.P53   1997
     294.5'513--dc21   96-36849

Llewellyn Publications
A Division of Llewellyn Worldwide, Ltd.
P.O. Box 64383, Dept. K522-3, St. Paul, MN 55164-0383

Dedication

This book is dedicated to Cheryl, my best friend, wife, and the mother of our divine daughter.

Acknowledgments

To Alice Christensen, I am most thankful for inviting me to join her on a grand adventure that would eventually lead to meeting his eminence, Swami Lakshmanjoo, and for her helpful suggestions during the writing of this book. Thanks also to Mike Van Winkle, a friend, a student of Kashmir Shaivism, and, through our many discussions, a contributor to this text. Many thanks to Patricia Rockwood for taking interest in this book and helping with the editing. A special thanks to Laurie Rosin for organizing the original material that went into this text and helping with the editing.

Contents

Swami Lakshmanjoo
May 7, 1907–September 27, 1991

The Five Acts of God
To Create
To Protect and Maintain
To Destroy
To Conceal Himself
To Reveal Himself

What does this mean to us as individual human beings?

A Note from the Author

IN THE FIELD OF SPIRITUALITY, THERE ARE THOSE WHO, IN A SINGLE LIFE-time, find enlightenment and realize who and what they are. Others come and go through many lives, up and down in their spiritual growth, and eventually, by the grace of God, come face to face with the Supreme.

This book is about starting at the bottom and working your way up, moving from a gross existence to one of increasing spiritual refinement. I hope you become as inspired by this great knowledge as I have.

Sincerely,

J. R. Picken

Om Namah Shivaya
Om to You, Oh Lord Siva
Om to You, Oh Great Bhairava; the Destroyer of the Individual Ego
Om to You, Oh Creator/Protector/Destroyer

The Symbol for Divinity and the Mantra Om (AUM in Sanskrit)
The primeval vibration out of which all else manifests

Om Namah Shivaya
(Om! To Siva I bow)

This all-powerful Divinity dwells as the living essence in all things—any object, any living creature, any action, any quality, can be taken as the image of divinity and worshipped as such. Those who are wise bow to everything, calling it God.

To You
Om Namah Shivaya

Preface

YOU HOLD IN YOUR HANDS A PRICELESS TREASURE, THE KEY TO SELF-understanding—a self-understanding that goes beyond your wildest imagination. In this book, you will discover a philosophy that will help you create a new and more empowered way of life. This philosophy is powerful because it answers those timeless questions: *Who am I?*, *What am I?*, and *What is my relationship to the divine?* For most people, these questions remain a mystery, because very few know the answers. These ultimate truths have been lost or kept secret through the ages and only a handful of the greatest sages have passed them by word of mouth to their students over the millennia.

All this is about to change. There is nothing more exciting or powerful than discovering the wonderful truths about yourself. The information in this book will shatter your old self-image and lay the groundwork for a new one. By the grace of Swami Lakshmanjoo, the answers to the ancient secrets have become available to any who are interested. This knowledge is a boon to the world like no other, the ultimate gift by the grace of God.

According to Lakshmanjoo, humanity is at the end of an era of gradual decay into complete and utter ignorance, where people have completely forgotten who they are. This greatest of all teachers has shattered this ignorance with divine knowledge and personally ushered humanity into its new beginning.

Lakshmanjoo's teaching is called Kashmir Shaivism. The Shaiva philosophy is perhaps the most ancient system of thought in the world. It is not a religion but a heightened awareness of yourself and how you interact with your world. Although the philosophy has been around for centuries, its principles have been passed along only by word of mouth and were nearly lost several times.

Detailed texts about Kashmir Shaivism exist from ancient times. The philosophy was clearly outlined and committed to paper in the ninth century A.D. by two prolific writers: the master Abhinavagupta and his disciple Ksemaraja. Recently, scholars translated their volumes verbatim from Sanskrit into English, preserving the exactness of the authors' meanings and beliefs. Advanced practitioners of Kashmir Shaivism prize these books, and those with great knowledge of this system of thought consider them an asset. Unfortunately, the texts hold little value for beginners, who know nothing of God or of themselves.

Lakshmanjoo, my own teacher, wrote two books: *Kashmir Shaivism: The Secret Supreme* (Universal Shaiva Trust, 1985) and *Lectures on Practice and Discipline in Kashmir Shaivism* (Universal Shaiva Trust, 1982). Both, however, are extremely complex, unfamiliar to the Western way of thinking, and filled with concepts that are totally foreign. These books, too, would be of little use to the novice.

Preface

No books about Kashmir Shaivism have existed for the beginner—until now. *Creator, Protector, Destroyer* is the first. In this book, you will find the fundamental aspects of Kashmir Shaivism, my interpretation of them, and explanations of how I applied them to my own life as a beginner in this grand adventure.

Most of what I learned comes from five sources: (1) Lakshmanjoo, the living essence of this philosophy and my inspiration, a person who taught me directly during my visits to his home in India; (2) Lakshmanjoo's books; (3) videotaped lectures given by Lakshmanjoo and recorded by John Hughes plus Hughes' book, *Self-Realization in Kashmir Shaivism: The Oral Teachings of Swami Lakshmanjoo* (State University of New York Press, 1994); (4) the modern translations of the original works of Abhinavagupta and Ksemaraja by several different scholars; and (5) lectures given by Lakshmanjoo and recorded by Alice Christensen and subsequently transcribed.

As a disciple of Swami Lakshmanjoo, I consider myself an interpreter, a go-between for him and you so his teachings can be brought into a realm that novices can understand and use.

The transformation of my life and my never-ending adventure began in 1977 when I met Alice Christensen, executive director and founder of the American Yoga Association. She introduced me to the intriguing philosophy called Kashmir Shaivism and to Swami Lakshmanjoo, that teaching's last living master.

After I met Swami Lakshmanjoo in 1981, I developed an intense urge to write a book. I had never thought about writing before, and the only subjects I knew anything about were medicine and physiology. I decided to focus on the medical and physiological consequences of bad habits such as smoking, taking drugs, and drinking alcohol.

CREATOR, PROTECTOR, DESTROYER

Soon my aspiration became a preoccupation. I worked on this project for a year, writing every day. Insidiously, new thoughts—not of physiology but of philosophy—filled my head. I found myself overwhelmed by an almost fanatical obsession but did not connect my impulse to write with the unfamiliar teaching I was struggling so hard to understand.

At first I was confused by my lessons in Kashmir Shaivism. The ideas were incongruent with what I already knew, and I tried in vain to create a new outlook on life. Even though I was learning more and more, the puzzle pieces had yet to fit into a clear or simple picture. Every day I wrote and wrote and wrote, trying to sort out the concepts. Every day I became more frustrated.

Then one morning, thousands of pages later, I woke up, bolted upright in bed, and at that instant saw the whole picture as clear as a perfect diamond crystal. It was suddenly so simple!

From that morning forward, everything changed. It was a miracle! Everything looked different. I could understand why I was the way I was, why my parents, my wife, and all of humanity were the way they were. I comprehended that how we picture ourself and who we really are are two totally different concepts and that this misconception is the cause of our suffering and pain.

Unfortunately, my new insight did not help my state of being. In fact, I grew even more agitated because I could not figure out how to communicate my newfound wisdom. I knew what I wanted to say, but I could not capture it in my writing.

In 1991, the last time I saw Lakshmanjoo, I set at his feet a notebook filled with what I had written. I had never said a word to him about my awful frustration. He died shortly thereafter, and my notebook was returned to me by one of his devotees.

Then, almost a complete wreck, I sat down to write once again— but something was different. I liked my work! The phrasing seemed better, closer to the mark. I sent the first twenty pages to my typist, and she put a note in with the invoice: "This is really something!" I knew I was on my way.

Over the years, my wife and I spent many evenings and late nights talking about this philosophy and the impact it has had on our lives. It is the content of these discussions that I have captured on paper.

John R. Picken
Florida
April 1996

Introduction

WHAT IS THE MOST WONDERFUL, USEFUL ASSET IN THE WORLD? Power—the power to make things in your life happen the way you want them to, from the most important to the least significant event. This is what I want.

What would I do with more personal power? Would I choose to be healthy and fit, happy and brimming with self-confidence? Would I opt for a harmonious environment at home, true love in my marriage, a happy child with high self-esteem? Of course I would.

A few years ago, however, I was helpless to make these dreams come true. At home, in the workplace, and in the community I was struggling just to survive. In spite of my best intentions and efforts, I faltered in nearly every resolve. A very sad predicament, indeed, especially since almost all of humanity is similarly plagued.

What I learned can stop this cycle of failure, which leads to self-disgust and self-hatred and poisons every aspect of our existence. The first step in stopping this cycle is to learn the facts about who we are, because our self-concept sets the tone for our life. What we believe ourself to be is what we become.

At the beginning of my journey, I realized that I knew nothing about my true nature. My past view, based on superstition and ignorance, focused on evil, sin, and weakness. It presumed that I was innately flawed. For me, this antiquated message promoted self-hatred and a predictable attitude and behavior that now appears to me as something quite ugly—even grotesque. All this changed when I began to realize the power of changing my outlook about myself and the world to reflect a bigger picture that could answer the questions *Who am I?* and *What am I?*

I am inviting you to change your identity, as I have, and build personal power in a way you never thought possible.

For the first time ever, you stand on the threshold of an adventure like no other. This is the beginning of the journey into the center of your own wondrous self. It is a spiritual journey, where science and spirituality meet at the same point, inside the self.

Many people claim to be religious, meaning that they believe in the basic creeds of their faith. This is well and good and serves a beneficial purpose for humanity. Religion evolves from the collective moral and ethical principles of a people, defining how they live according to the dictates of a higher power, a power that supersedes the force and might of mortals and judges their acts. The divine figureheads (such as Jesus or Mohammed) of these religions professed these principles and lived them as an example to their followers.

Besides acknowledging a higher power, all religions define good and evil and essentially believe that salvation comes by the grace of a divine power (such as God or Allah), are dependent on one's behavior, and come about by the strength of one's personal faith. These teachings have had an incredibly powerful effect on humankind. These basic tenets of religion are good, as far as they go, but they are in themselves powerless to ultimately answer the questions Who am I? and What am I? There is more, infinitely more; all religion does is serve humanity at its most mundane, superficial, and worldly level. There is nothing in these teachings that can elevate the individual above this worldly domain.

Religion is not spirituality in the purest sense of the word as I will use it in this book. The way I see it, spirituality has only to do with the individual, the search for self-discovery in the here and now, and how this discovery relates to God.

In my opinion, religion primarily gives people identity to share with others in valued customs and traditions—a social solidarity that comforts and sustains. Many gain great strength and solace from their belief in a higher power and their observance of the traditions of their faith. But, although practical in times of need, these beliefs are seldom developed beyond a mere survival mechanism in coping with the unforgiving nature of daily reality.

It is very important for you to understand that the concepts contained within this book are not intended to replace your present religious beliefs or customs. On the contrary, the intent is to add to them. What you will gain after reading this book is a broader understanding of who you are and what you are. The specific customs, rituals, and moral commandments of your religious background are wonderful—hang on to them. But there is a much bigger picture of something now hidden, and this bigger picture is what we are after. The philosophy outlined in this book will add something more to who you are, not take something away.

The adventure of self-realization in spirituality is an adventure like no other—it's one that goes beyond our usual everyday existence. In this adventure, the zeal is for more than simple survival; the goal is to unravel the mystery of the self that lies hidden, just out of reach.

If you are intrigued by this idea, you must realize that discovering the mystery of the self is no ordinary journey. It cannot be made by those who are unfit, mentally or physically. It requires clarity of mind and top physical health. Spirituality is the ultimate quest, and this is the best reason to want to be healthy and fit, clear-minded and strong. Reading this book is the beginning of an adventure that will extend your faith in the divine into the realm of personally understanding the ultimate secret, the nature of your own self.

It is unlikely that you—or your life—will ever be the same after reading this book. By the grace of God and Lakshmanjoo, this supreme knowledge is now available to any and all. I am inviting you to change your identity as I have done and build personal power in a way you never thought possible.

This book represents a journal of my own conceptualizations pertaining to the ancient philosophy of Shaivism and how I have applied these ideas in a practical way to my daily living. Although my intent is to share this supreme science with others, I am speaking not only to you but to myself, providing a gentle reminder of what I have learned and what I need to practice. A philosophy is worthless unless you can remember what you are working toward; I remember by writing, reading, contemplating, rewriting, and then reading again.

Chapter One

The Search for Meaning

ONE OF MY EARLIEST MEMORIES IS PLUNKING PENNIES, NICKELS, AND dimes into my piggy bank to save money for my college education. According to my parents, education meant liberation, the road to happiness, the guarantee of self-fulfillment. They fantasized about the gifts the world would lay at my feet. I listened to them talking about a new world, a changing world, one where education and sophistication were the tickets to success.

That early programming had a tremendous effect and, without question, when the time came, I went to college. My psyche had been programmed to believe that happiness was locked up in the libraries of Washington State University. Like everyone else, I searched for self-fulfillment, ready to turn all my fantasies into reality so I could live happily ever after.

CREATOR, PROTECTOR, DESTROYER

Because my high school graduating class had only forty-five students, I knew everybody. I was popular. Washington State University, on the other hand, had about twelve thousand students, and I was Mr. Nobody. I felt inferior, inadequate, shy, and I hated myself. I felt frustrated in every way. I realized that the happiness and success my parents had promised me were not going to be found at Washington State University. I had to push on to something bigger and better—something major. I decided to go to medical school and become a scientist and physician.

I will always remember waiting to board the plane that would take me from my home in Washington state to Cleveland, Ohio, to begin medical school. My parents were proud, but I was nervous. At the ripe old age of twenty-two, I had committed myself to going a thousand miles away from all that was familiar to me. I felt the future looming over me as if I were about to parachute behind enemy lines.

Case Western Reserve University is situated on the demarcation line between Cleveland's suburbs and its downtown ghetto. On the same side of the street as the graduate house where I lived, and just two storefronts down, were drug dealing, prostitution, peep shows, violence, and death. On the other side of the street, scholars had earned several Nobel prizes and people talked about lives in research and education and frequented foreign-film theaters and fine restaurants.

I never got used to the proximity of these two diametrically opposed worlds that faced the same avenue. I used to stand on the front steps of my building and wonder whether all those poor people milling around out there on the street felt as lost and displaced as I did. I didn't have a good night's sleep for months. I called my parents to tell them I wanted to come home. They persuaded me to finish the first semester. I agreed begrudgingly, just to keep the peace.

Fortunately things began to change. I became a city boy, competing with the best of them for grades and women. I started to feel the jubilation of the conqueror. I felt invincible. I had no doubt that, after graduating with two doctoral degrees, I could step out on the swimming pool in the gymnasium and walk across the water. The emphasis my parents had put on education when I was a child had created a fantasy that was almost magical.

But beneath that fantasy, the fear of not transforming myself into someone special drove me through long days and nights of study, year after year.

Even though I and my fellow students concentrated on our education, the real drama in our lives, the thing we talked about morning, noon, and night, was love. I learned a lot during those years—more about life than about medicine. The truth about human interaction staggered my mind. I learned that relationships are as powerfully brutal as they are ecstatic. Love and hate seemed equally intense: making up and breaking up, from ecstasy to total devastation. For a long time it didn't make sense to me how two people could give each other so much pleasure and so much pain at the same time.

Gradually my euphoria faded. I had proven that I was intelligent, hardworking, resourceful, dedicated, creative, and studious. I knew an incredible amount about the human body. I had everything I needed for a brilliant career. I had friends and good times, and every door was open to me in the medical world I had chosen—but that was not enough. Despite a thin veneer of sophistication, I still felt horribly incomplete. My education had somehow failed me. I had believed from the bottom of my heart in a fantasy that becoming a doctor would make me complete, powerful, and happy. It had not! I noticed that whatever I achieved would never be enough. I felt defeat rather than jubilation. I was still the same ol'

John R. Picken. To come this far, only to find out that happiness was not waiting for me rolled up in my diplomas, was a crushing blow.

Once this revelation became clear to me, I began noticing an undercurrent of dissatisfaction in those around me. Everybody suffered from the same predicament. Even those eminent professors and scientists whom I revered so highly seemed disappointed, as if their own truth, happiness, and fulfillment were just out of reach, around the next corner, or at the end of the next experiment. Our goals of love ever after, happy children, and personal fulfillment were illusions. What we hoped for, worked for, and believed in and what actually happened to us in our life were two different things.

I wanted to understand why that was true. Why did I feel and act the way I did? Why was there such a discrepancy between my beliefs, fantasies, and ideals and my real life? Why was I filled with love and hate? I felt there must be a unifying wisdom that connects everything neatly into a framework upon which all else was built. I felt confident that after I had discovered that great knowledge, my life would be fixed.

Remarkably, I have done just that. I have discovered that Truth and invite you to share it with me, as a great master halfway around the world passed his wisdom to many, including a small, fortunate group of Americans, of which I was a member. You may be shocked and thrilled by the simplicity and profundity of what you have already started to learn regarding your true nature. You will be able to cast aside feelings of isolation, loneliness, and powerlessness. From this point forward, life can be totally different.

My real education began in 1977. I was on my way to Irv's, a student hangout. Breakfast at Irv's on Saturday and Sunday was a ritual for me. As I walked along, I noticed a poster in the window of a vegetarian restaurant, advertising a trip to India to study Yoga. There was a telephone number but no other information. In the seventies, everybody was trying to "find themselves," and Eastern philosophy was one popular avenue. I made the phone call and was invited to an afternoon tea where I met several members of the Light of Yoga Society and heard more about the itinerary.

I didn't learn many specifics from that afternoon get-together, but the trip seemed exotic and different. I could afford it; as a graduate instructor, I had just received $3,500—more money than I'd ever seen in one lump sum—for teaching part of a dental physiology course. I had already paid for my medical tuition and room and board, so I could do anything I wanted with the money.

I paid my money, and at the end of June I met up with a group of sixty strangers at JFK International Airport in New York. Six people were in charge; the others seemed as lost as I was. We boarded a Boeing 747 and were on our way.

Thirty-two hours later, we reached New Delhi. Jet lag, nearly twelve hours' worth, turned my biological clock upside down. The country was at the beginning of its monsoon season, the temperature was a hundred degrees, and the humidity was ninety percent. I didn't know it was possible to feel so lousy physically. Unfortunately, the hard traveling was still ahead. At that time the New Delhi International Airport was a one-room, 1920s flight hangar with no air conditioning. Unloading three hundred people and checking them single file through customs required several hours. None of us had taken a shower in the last day and a half, and with the heat, humidity, and sticky perspiration, I felt as if I were swimming in my shirt and slacks. By the time we left the airport, everyone was bone weary and disoriented.

Several cabs took our group from the airport to our hotel in the city. As I gazed though the cab window, the people appeared strange and

5

different from anyone I had ever known. They were small, and everyone wore what seemed to be nightclothes: loose-fitting cotton pants and shirts. Most unsettling of all were the piercing eyes that followed us everywhere we went.

The Oberoi Hotel, left behind by the British aristocracy, had undoubtedly been fancy in its heyday but had since deteriorated into a smelly, dingy place, with thick mildew in the carpet and walls. The mattress on my bed felt damp. My body ached, and jet lag discouraged sleep. I had come for enlightenment but instead had found hell. We were strangers in a strange land.

We spent two nights in New Delhi before starting the last leg of our journey. We reluctantly returned to the airport—this time to the domestic terminal—and waited half a day to board an Airbus that flew us north into Kashmir, a province of India that borders Pakistan, Tibet, Sinkiang (a region in China), and a short stretch of Afghanistan.

In 1946, when India won independence from England, the maharaja of Kashmir was given a choice of whether to ally himself with Pakistan or India. For several months, he could not make up his mind between the two countries. Meanwhile, rebels from Pakistan crossed into the maharaja's principality and advanced toward the capital city of Srinagar, looting, raping, and slaughtering as they went. When Lord Mountbatten, governor general of the new Indian Dominion, learned of the situation, he offered to defend Kashmir on the condition that the maharaja immediately accede to the new Indian state. The maharaja agreed the next day. Forty-eight hours later, Mountbatten made good on his word and sent a battalion of Indian regulars to Srinagar. Neither his army nor the rebels were able to make headway, however, and the front became the western edge of a cease-fire line. To this day part of what was once Kashmir is now in Pakistan, while the majority of present-day Kashmir is controlled by India.

Even in 1977 there was tremendous political unrest between this northern state and bordering countries. Our destination was the capital city, and we found Srinagar's airport filled with armed military personnel. Everywhere we turned, we saw soldiers with rifles or machine guns slung over their shoulders. It was a frightening experience. None of the military personnel looked friendly, especially to the American tourists in brightly colored hiking outfits. I'm sure a number of the soldiers thought we'd be good for target practice, if nothing else. The civilians stared at us intently, with chilling looks. As in so many corners of the world, this chapter in Indian history may never be over. The streets in the towns and villages of the Kashmir valley continue to flow with blood—a never-ending flow.

As we approached Srinagar, we saw Dal Lake. The city was situated at one end of the lake, and little communities and trading posts were scattered along its entire length. Dal Lake is about twenty miles long, three to four miles wide at its greatest width, and quite shallow. On one edge of the lake close to Srinagar rested vast communities of vegetable growers. These farmers lived right on the lake itself, on little islands that stretched off a multitude of small channelways. In the open, undisturbed areas of the lake, vast fields of lotus petals floated on the water's surface, protecting and cupping their beautiful inner blooms.

We drove straight through the town and onto the lake's perimeter. About five miles down shore was a small, manmade causeway that extended several hundred yards into the lake, and along it was a string of six houseboats. These were to be home for sixty people during the next month.

Actually, the accommodations were very nice because they were removed from the activity and commotion of Srinagar and protected from the elements. Each houseboat was about fifty feet long and twenty feet wide, big enough for a living room, dining room, and four small bedrooms. No cooking was done on the boats; a mess area was established in the middle of the peninsula where the food for the entire camp was prepared by several Kashmiris who had learned to cater to American tastes.

Life started to improve. I adjusted to the jet lag and unfamiliar environment. With other group members, I ventured into the town to explore the area and shop. Srinagar covers an area of six to eight square miles; its main export is Kashmir rugs, woven in attics by children and old men and women whose giant weaving looms are wedged between struts and roof supports, leaving hardly any room to move.

Besides these excursions into the city, there wasn't much to do except lie back and enjoy the natural wonders of the area. Dal Lake sits in a large valley around which the mountains rise abruptly. These are the foothills of the Himalayas; the surrounding peaks rise to twenty thousand feet. Behind these hills, the earth's crust lies nakedly exposed; fractured into giant pieces and snow-covered year-round, the mountains shoot upward in every direction. It was mesmerizing to see something so gigantic poking up out of nowhere. I could tell one piece of the earth's crust from another because of the direction of the exposed layers and clearly apparent detail. I have never seen anything like it again. On a geological time scale, these mountains are brand new.

Whenever we slowly paddled up and down these channels, I watched children playing or bathing, young girls washing clothes, and others just gazing into the distance. Their whole life existed on the edge of those banks.

After we were settled in, the camp leaders focused on our daily routine and Yoga classes. I had no idea what any of this was all about. *Yoga?* I asked myself. *What is Yoga, anyway?*

Each day we were taught Yoga postures and exercises called *asans,* then we meditated. At lunch and dinner, the houseboat leaders led discussions on philosophical ideas. It was all incomprehensible to me. Whenever a group of us met after a lecture, I was always amazed by how each person interpreted the material in a completely different way, as if we had attended separate programs. I didn't learn much during that first trip.

I went back to India in 1981. I convinced my new wife, Cheryl, to come with me. This time we were going on a new adventure into the Himalayas. The plan was to travel on horseback: three days in, three days out, straight up the side of the mountains. Our destination was Amarnath, the sacred site of pilgrimage for thousands of years. Whole villages or extended families often take up a collection to send just one person on this spiritual journey; they believe that this effort blesses not only the villagers and immediate family but those for generations to come.

The path we traveled was only two feet wide on a straight up-and-down cliffside. The summit we breasted was 14,500 feet high and breathing was difficult. Because young and old were part of our group, portable oxygen tanks were available so everyone could manage the final ascent on foot. As we neared the end of our journey, sleetlike rain soaked us to the bone, and everybody was near hysteria, including me. We were cold, demoralized, and hungry.

That night, covered with mud, we huddled in our sleeping bags and thought about being back home in our own bed in the United States. It seemed as if we were on an insane adventure for no good reason.

But that was before I met a man like no other.

Amarnath is a huge recess in the side of a giant mountain; every year, thirty thousand pilgrims from all over India visit the site. An unusual ice formation, similar to an inverted stalactite, projects up from the center of the floor of an enormous overhang. The frozen configuration remains there year-round, even during the intense heat of summertime. According to legend, this lingam (a symbolic male phallus, representing the creative force of the universe) marks the spot where Siva, god of the universe, and his wife, Parvati, passed from physical form into spiritual formlessness, the highest state of universal consciousness. Most great yogis travel to Amarnath at least once during their lifetime. Unfortunately, at the time this upside-down icicle didn't mean anything to me—I wasn't in a very contemplative mood. As I sat before it, my only concerns were climbing on my horse and getting back into my sleeping bag.

After our return from Amarnath, Swami Lakshmanjoo visited our camp. There was a stateliness about this old man in the way he walked, in his gestures, in his smile. He was positively radiant. In spite of his many years, he was very handsome, with light brown skin and short, evenly cut hair. The focal point of his physical being, though, was his eyes. Dark and beautiful, they somehow conveyed to me the feeling that the meaning of life and the truth of my own existence were right there, behind those eyes.

I had heard about this man before; Swami Lakshmanjoo was a recognized spiritual master over the entirety of India and was the most famous person in Kashmir. Whenever he went out, people recognized him immediately and treated him with great respect. Awestruck, people crowded around him and asked for favors or blessings. Everybody wanted something from Lakshmanjoo.

Today, however, he was not feeling well and had heard there was an American doctor in our group. He wanted me to examine him. That afternoon was the beginning of my new life.

I had preconceived notions about how it would feel to meet him, but the effect he had on me was unlike anything I had ever imagined. This was no ordinary man. There was something about his eyes that radiated compassion and understanding of the human predicament. He didn't have to say a word; it was just there on his face.

Lakshmanjoo's parents were of the local aristocracy. His father owned the business that built all the beautiful houseboats on Dal Lake. Just before his birth, many of the great sages from the surrounding area came to Lakshmanjoo's home and told his parents that a great entity was about to be born. As a child, Lakshmanjoo was treated like a god.

By Kashmiri standards he was well-to-do, in a position to live humbly but comfortably. He accepted no money or any type of payment for his teachings. His messages were insights regarding humanity's relationship to God.

Some deep, untapped part of my being understood that whatever Lakshmanjoo was, it was so massive that it transcended ordinary comprehension. Just being in his presence, I knew that something was happening to me that would last for the rest of my life. I desperately wanted to know everything he had to offer.

I returned to India five more times after 1981, each time to sit at the feet of this enlightened master and listen to his lessons about the meaning of life and God. He was capable of giving me the answers to the questions *What am I?* and *Who am I?* In the oral tradition of Kashmir Shaivism, Lakshmanjoo was the last living master in a line of philosophers that dated back to before the time of Abhinavagupta in the ninth century A.D.

Over the years, I found that the journeys never became easier. About six to eight weeks before each departure, an undercurrent of anticipation would unsettle every aspect of my life. In spite of this—not to mention physical discomfort, fatigue, mental confusion, and culture shock—I went. In my heart I knew that something tremendously important awaited me halfway around the world.

On our last trip, we followed our usual routine, although tension was etched on our faces. No one had heard from Lakshmanjoo over the winter. The man was in his early eighties, and we were all concerned for his health.

In previous years, Lakshmanjoo received us in the late afternoon. This visit was no exception; he would see us the next day at 5:30 P.M. We unpacked our bags, tidied our accommodations, sprayed for bugs, dusted, filtered drinking water, had a late-night meal, and went to bed.

The next morning we woke early and worked on the camp all day. Again we dusted and sprayed with insecticide—although we did more damage to ourselves than to the spiders—and by late afternoon we were exhausted and nauseated. We washed up and got ready to see our spiritual guide.

To get to Lakshmanjoo's home, we drove over a small mountain down to a lakeshore, which we followed for five miles. I knew every bump and turn; every day at home back in the United States I had thought about this trip.

Lakshmanjoo's living quarters were on a hillside overlooking Dal Lake. George and John, Australians who were two of Lakshmanjoo's devotees, received us. We waited anxiously a few minutes in front of his teahouse, and then he appeared. As usual, I was in a state of total anticipatory awe and fear. He looked much stronger than I had expected. A smile lit his face; he was luminous.

We followed Lakshmanjoo into his teahouse, a verandah with a large, flat couch in one corner and places to sit or kneel at its base. He seemed ecstatic and was talkative and completely clear mentally. He told us that during the winter he had gone into a semicomatose state, which had lasted for many weeks. John and George had sat beside him during this entire time, doing what they could for him, wondering whether he was going to live or die. Interestingly, it was not illness from which Lakshmanjoo had suffered but his transition from his worldly state into the divine.

He said that when this great passage takes place, one becomes breathless and without a pulse. Even though the body's functions essentially stop, the spirit supports the body during this divine transition.

Lakshmanjoo explained that he barely made it through this transformation because of modern medical science. One night, four years earlier, his heart slowed almost to a stop while he was in a trance. Somebody took his pulse and panicked. His caregiver did not understand what was happening and refused to listen to Lakshmanjoo's protests that he was all right. The master was flown to Delhi for a cardiac evaluation, which eventually led to a pacemaker insertion.

Lakshmanjoo explained that the placement of this pacemaker could have been the end of a whole lifetime of work. To make the final and ultimate leap into supreme Siva-hood, the heart and the breath must stop. Through the entire winter of 1988–1989, Lakshmanjoo, semiconscious, struggled toward the ultimate transformation in spite of his pacemaker, which kicked on automatically when his heart rate dropped below sixty beats per minute. He explained that the force of his spirit had overridden the electronics of the pacemaker, allowing him to accomplish the impossible!

The last night we were with Lakshmanjoo in India I told him that he looked more beautiful than I had ever seen him before. With a big smile on his face he said that it was the divine now that was supporting his body. He was radiant.

As I knelt in awe before him, I wondered exactly what transformation he had undergone. He possessed more vitality and energy than I'd ever known him to have over the last ten years.

He told us that for one such as he, there was a right time to die; but that in a dream his master had told him he could die whenever he chose to—any time was good now. He explained that he had become "fully realized." The only reason for him to stay on this earthly plane was to help this planet and its inhabitants. Because of his infinite compassion and understanding of the human predicament, he was laying the groundwork for all humanity.

Lakshmanjoo was finishing a journey that he had started long before. I was a novice. The message he had for me and so many others that he affected in India and all over the world was how to begin this same spiritual path. As a novice, I knew I might not reach his exalted position—at least not in this lifetime—but what he had to offer could transform even the lowest of the low.

I believe that as soon as most of the world's illumined individuals have found what they want, they remove themselves from this earthly plane. Only the greatest of the great, the true teachers of humanity, stay behind out of mercy and offer guidance to those who want to learn. Undoubtedly, that is why I was there. I was looking for something that Lakshmanjoo was willing to give. If there was ever a person who was genuinely kind and empathic, it was he. As I sat humbly, listening and trying to comprehend, I understood in my heart that above all else I wanted to know and feel what he knew and felt.

Making eye contact with this great man was an experience like no other. I realized that I was in the presence of a great and powerful being. As I sat at his feet and looked up, our eyes met and locked, and he gazed into the very essence of my being. I am not sure what he saw, but I think he was rearranging me from the inside out, changing my destiny. (For years my wife and I had been without children. When Lakshmanjoo found out how much we wanted a child, he said he would take care of it.

Shortly afterward, my wife became pregnant and our beautiful baby, Amanda, was born. Her birth was a miracle.)

Lakshmanjoo understood what and who he was. His behavior was impeccable. No matter what, in every circumstance, he was uplifting to those around him. He was the living example of the philosophy he taught to those who were interested. He was the only person I ever knew who was pure compassion. No anger or violence leaked from his being. Everything that came from him was inspiring, sweet, and nurturing. He explained that God is not a being but a state of being.

By sheer will he controlled his actions and speech. He told me that his will was greater than that of anyone who had ever lived on this planet. It was so powerful, he had totally and completely subjugated nature in his own self. This was a person who stood on top of the forces of the universe.

That year, 1989, was the last time I went to India. Civil war broke out in Kashmir between the Hindus and the Muslims, and foreigners were no longer safe in that isolated, hostile area.

My companions and I agonized about whether we would ever see Lakshmanjoo again. We heard nothing from him for long periods of time.

In April 1991 we heard that Lakshmanjoo had arrived in Los Angeles and was staying with John and Denise Hughes. They were also devotees of this great man and had studied under and lived with him for a number of years in India. Their youngest child, a son, Veresh, was born while John and Denise were living with Lakshmanjoo. They had since returned to their home in the United States. John and Denise notified Lakshmanjoo's devotees that he was with them. Because we had not been able to get to him, he had come to us. He had traveled halfway around the world to visit us one last time. He wanted to see everybody. We were amazed and excited. I was especially thrilled because I would be able to bring my wife and daughter.

CREATOR, PROTECTOR, DESTROYER

Lakshmanjoo was gratified to see little Amanda, whom he introduced to new arrivals as his daughter. He said that she was not created in
the ordinary way. He claimed that he had created her, and she was therefore his. "I am her father," he said. Later that year, on September 27, Lakshmanjoo died.

I cannot begin to imagine the total effect Lakshmanjoo had on all of
us. Now he will begin to influence you, your family, and your world.

As my own wisdom developed through the grace of this extraordinary man, the shocking truth became clearer and clearer: We are not what
we think we are in any way, shape, or form.

Lakshmanjoo said that the future would hold great change, that
humanity was at the bottom of an era and ready to move into the new. He
explained that dwelling in the past must cease. "Don't look back," he said.
"Pretend that the past never existed!"

Saddling up for another day's ride on the way to Amarnath in Kashmir.

Amarnath travelers take advantage of a sunny afternoon to dry clothes.

*Evening in Panchatarni, elevation about 10,000 feet,
the last stop before reaching Amarnath.*

*The final leg of
the journey to
Amarnath.*

The cave of Amarnath, high in the Himalayas in Kashmir.

View from a houseboat on Dal Lake in Srinagar, Kashmir.

19

The teahouse in Kashmir where Lakshmanjoo received guests and devotees.

*Lakshmanjoo intent
on teaching,
around 1987.*

*Amanda playing
dress-up.*

*Amanda with Lakshmanjoo in April
1991, during his visit to the U.S.*

Amanda at 3½, with her mother Cheryl.

Lakshmanjoo in his teahouse in Kashmir, around 1986.

Chapter Two

One Reason for Existing

ACCORDING TO KASHMIR SHAIVISM, THE PURPOSE FOR HAVING A BODY is to discover God, to achieve a personal experience of the divine. There is no other purpose or higher calling for being here. This reality is a stage set for achieving this end, prearranged and orchestrated by God Himself—a divine drama. From this single concept comes the meaning of life and the realization of what is important and what is not.

For the wise, the drama of life becomes an instrument for the single purpose of achieving self-realization. Life, for those who understand, takes on direction and meaning. For those who do not understand or do not care, life has no meaning. These people are filled with depression, despair, and fear; they experience chronic stress and confusion of the mind that has no solution; their lives are tortured.

Throughout time, many spiritual aspirants have denounced this existence and withdrawn from it. They also achieve nothing. Why is this so? Because the stage itself, this whole world, this whole existence, is divine. Every speck of it—every piece of dirt, the rocks, the moon, the stars, animals, human beings, even thoughts and feelings, good and bad, evil and virtuous, from the highest to the most unmentionable lowest—if it exists, it is divine. This whole reality is an unfolding of the divine. To denounce it would lead to a dead end for those individuals seeking self-realization.

According to Kashmir Shaivism, only one thing exists—God. There is no other thing or living being here or anywhere else that exists—just God, totally alone, the Existent One. Everything is God! Shaiva legend states that God, in order to enjoy the enormity of His own glamour and power, created another perspective, a multitude of universes, to appreciate His own self. In His supreme state of being, there was no vantage point of comparison. Of course there was nothing higher, and in this state of singularity there is nothing lower either, only the supreme "I AM" and His Energy. So, out of His own Self, out of this point of singularity, He created time, space, matter, and life.

Of the utmost importance in understanding this supreme philosophy is this—God is not separate from what He creates, God is what he creates. God becomes His own creations. Now, once God has created the universe He not only exists as "I AM," but also as "I AM THAT"—THAT being everything created. Everything is made out of God: dirt, rocks, the moon, the sun, stars, animals, human beings. Therefore all the individual beings, all the actors and actresses (you and me) in this divine drama, are literally the Existent One. Most intriguing and setting the stage for a drama like no other, God purposefully makes it such that He forgets who He is while existing in this self-imposed, limited state of being. He becomes lost in a state of total ignorance and vulnerability.

What could be more exciting than being God and not knowing that you are God? To be God and not know that you are God is the essence of this game of intrigue and excitement and the reason for this existence and the players that fill it. It is from this perspective of limitation that God (we as limited beings) ultimately rediscovers who He really is. It is stated that at that instant of self-recognition, God realizes he always knew who He was. The whole charade is a trick of His own doing simply for the excitement and joy of this self-discovery, "I am That!" (meaning "I am this whole universe," "I am God!"). In other words, God creates the entire universe such that He can lose himself in it—vulnerable, ignorant, and unknowing of who he is—only so that He can ultimately find Himself again and, to His full glory, realize the magnitude of His splendor and beauty. This is the ultimate game, a game that only God can play.

To repeat, the purpose for having a body is to discover who we really are—the thrill, the excitement, the indescribable experience of self-realization; to be God and discover that while existing in the flesh. This is so profound it is almost incomprehensible; it is so simple it is almost unbelievable. This philosophy renders a supreme understanding to this single purpose and the meaning of life, and by definition renders all other philosophies and worldly pursuits meaningless. The next questions are *How do I attain this self-realization?* and *How do I implement this single purpose?* Until now, these secrets have been passed by word of mouth from master to disciple. By the grace of God and incarnated in His highest form, paraBhairava, Swami Lakshmanjoo has imparted to the world the formula for self-discovery.

The "how-to" in any pursuit requires an intellectual understanding of the principles involved, in this case philosophical/spiritual principles. An intellectual understanding of Kashmir Shaivism is absolutely necessary to achieve self-realization. This requires study in the same way you would attempt to master any other subject. Fortunately, enthusiasm and eventual love for this greatest of subjects leads to success, breaks through barriers of prior misconceptions, and allows for new ideas pertaining to God and one's own self.

In reality, this philosophy is about a love affair, a love affair like no other. This is a love affair between the limited being (you and me, i.e., God lost, vulnerable, and powerless) and the unlimited being (God or Lord Siva in His supreme state of being). Just as there is joy in the union between woman and man, the union between limited and unlimited gives rise to joy that is beyond comprehension. It is an experience in which the entire universe becomes one with the limited being, an experience of "I am all this!" It is an experience of total self-containment, total complete-ness, total freedom, and total power. It is the union of the Unlimited Being with the limited state of being. What is there to love but this? This is why God created this worldly drama—for this joy, for this love, for the worship of the divine, for this appreciation of His own magnificence and the playful game of getting there. There is no other purpose for being here except to pursue this love. Everything else leads to pain and suffering and confusion of the mind.

Although love becomes the final pathway to end this worldly adventure, there is more. How can we fall in love with something we do not understand? This is impossible. We must work out a framework of new ideas, new ways of looking at ourselves, and then make a connection with the divine. This does not come easily; it didn't for me—it takes time. On the other hand, understanding Kashmir Shaivism from an intellectual point of view alone leads nowhere except to a mind filled with divine ideas. Unfortunately, these divine ideas never lead to the experience of self-discovery. There is more required than understanding of metaphysical principles. Specific practices are required to lead to the mystical experience of knowing—of being—the Existent One. Thus the combination of principles and practices ultimately leads the aspirant to the doorstep of self-realization.

This grand adventure begins when a great teacher such as Lakshmanjoo explains to His devotees the secret of life and who they really are. Rather than a retreat from the world, this endeavor actually embraces the everyday world and becomes a testing ground for the measure of our devotion and strength—our commitment to this love affair. Even though aspirants continue to be of this world and perform their daily tasks, ultimately they must be completely absorbed in the single-minded pursuit of union with God; in actual fact, the rediscovery of their own self.

When this devotion turns into an obsession, we are well on the way. It is similar to the obsession that one experiences when young and in love, a state of mind where nothing else matters and the rest of the world is left behind. But this takes time. This kind of love comes later. There is much to do first. It goes without saying that it is impossible to fall in love with something that is hidden. I started by falling in love with the philosophy of Kashmir Shaivism and its greatest exponent, God incarnate in the body of Lakshmanjoo. This is the beginning, to open the door unto the world of divinity.

This book contains an introduction to Kashmir Shaivism and is written specifically for beginners. New students must understand the general principles of this philosophy and then begin to refine their way of life. To proceed in this adventure, the seeker of wisdom must live a moral and ethical existence and understand good and bad in a totally new framework. What this amounts to is the ABCs of spiritual pursuit, the basics. To overcome our state of limitation, ignorance, and vulnerability, this is a must, the first step. You cannot proceed without first becoming refined. Lord Siva in this limited state of being does good with one hand and bad with the other; this is the story of life for all of us. The challenge for the beginner is to take control of his or her own self. The principles and practices contained herein are what I have taken to heart and incorporated into my daily life, always working toward an ever-increasing refinement of my behavior.

The ultimate in self-realization is usually a process that takes several lifetimes once the aspirant is committed. Even though you may not achieve self-realization in a single lifetime, you can start on this journey and in the process become happy and content along the way, adding meaning, direction, and contentment such that the tragedy of life no longer exists. The process benefits yourself, your family, and the world in general. I can say from personal experience that all this is possible.

Chapter Three

Mistaken Identity

W E HUMANS, ALTHOUGH BLESSED WITH SELF-AWARENESS AND intellectual skills, are still babes in the woods when it comes to understanding ourselves. Not so long ago, we lived in caves and had just invented the wheel. When it comes to the complexities of human behavior, we think we know a lot, but we actually know very little.

Before we can accept the truth about ourselves, we must realize who we currently mistake ourselves to be—psychologically, sociologically, and theologically.

Modern psychologist-philosophers have had great difficulty trying to understand the human psyche. The real issue, though, is what it means to be conscious. The secrets of the universe depend on this answer! As will become readily evident as you continue with this book, we know about as much about consciousness as cave dwellers knew about nuclear physics.

Carl Jung and Sigmund Freud certainly knew there was much more to consciousness than could easily be explained, and what was beyond clear definition was termed the unconscious. These great scholars mistakenly believed that this part of our being was repressed, hidden, in the background. They knew that something profound rests in what they termed the unconscious, but exactly what, they did not know.

What is the real nature of being conscious? What is it, and who does it cause us to become? Even to the best scientific thinkers, the psyche remains an enigma, undefinable and unexplainable. The key to our behavior and our identity rests in knowing what it is to be conscious!

Mythology also points us in the right direction for unlocking our secret self. Myths are stories with roots in a culture's primitive folk beliefs, and myths with similar themes are found all over the world. These tales attempt to explain creation, divinity, and natural phenomena and to guess at the meaning of existence and death. A central theme in all mythologies is the journey of the hero or heroine. And where do they travel? They embark into the dangerous and forbidden unknown of the depths of consciousness, and it is here that they see truth and meaning for life. They return with personal power and wisdom. Mythology offers the theory that the secrets of nature lie inside our own being.

What or who were all of these theorists, scholars, and cultures past trying to comprehend and describe? Psychoanalytic theorists knew they were on to something, and mythology even more dramatically and in a much broader context describes the same incredible concept, something so massive that is beyond complete understanding; the message conveyed, therefore, is vague or incomplete.

It is a problem that has captured human attention as far back as we can know. *What am I? Who am I? What does it mean to be conscious?* The correct answers turn complexity and vagueness into simplicity. What we do not know is that the mystery we are trying to solve is standing in front of us in plain sight.

Except for the archetypal heroes (such as Jesus and Buddha), who personally made the journey into their own self and returned with great knowledge and self-understanding, the rest of us seem to be out in the cold, alone. It is difficult, if not impossible, for us to figure out our own initiation into this great adventure. That is the trouble with myths and religions; it is always someone else's adventure, never our own. We suffer from mistaken identity. As a starting point, let's take a quick look at who we are on the surface.

As we think about our life and strive to understand what sets us apart from animals, we proudly point to our ethical behavior and morality and the fact that we have a conscience and an ego. But morality and ethical behavior are nothing more than practical guidelines for social conduct. Typical socio-religious teachings outline the basics of how to become a social creature and live somewhat harmoniously with others, but that's all they do. They offer no real insight into the true composition of our nature. In my own case, even though I knew what was ethical, I didn't always live high-mindedly. We perceive ourselves to be civilized, highly refined beings. As individuals, we profess to be nonviolent. But we are mesmerized by sex and violence. In spite of what we want to believe about ourselves, psychologically we are sexual and violent beings. This is what holds our attention when we go to the movies, watch television, read romance novels, or turn on the news. We raise havoc in every aspect of our life—social, business, personal, and family; I certainly did. When it comes to the human psyche or, more specifically, human behavior, all we can do is throw up our hands and ask *Why?* When we have a model for good behavior, why don't we adhere to it? Why do we suffer so many problems with interpersonal relationships?

CREATOR, PROTECTOR, DESTROYER

It is easy to believe that our sexual and violent natures are some vestigial leftover from lower life, a throwback from the darkness that preceded the ascent of human beings. But this is not correct at all. Soon you will see that our sexual and violent natures are much more profound than this. Not to thoroughly understand these aspects of my own nature and bring these forces under control was a part of my downfall, part of this mistaken identity.

Our sexual and violent natures are more a part of our life than we could possibly imagine. One way or another, these two forces shatter our home, workplace, and the streets of the world. How about work at the office? Sexual harassment, back stabbing, ruthless manipulation, betrayal...wherever there are people, every conceivable underhanded maneuver is taking place. With our sexual and violent natures functioning out of control, we shatter the happiness and harmony in our home, workplace, and the planet. The terrible things we do to each other are beyond description. Every nook and cranny is filled with rage. The streets of the world are filled with rock throwing, machine gun fire, murder, and rape. Why? We are sexual and violent creatures, this is our nature! When I remember my own behavior, I shudder; but Lakshmanjoo told me, "Don't look back," and so I try not to.

Interesting as well as astonishing is the fact that the only way we can picture ourselves is as a wonderful person. This is not to say that we will not admit to shortcomings, but we insist that the true nature of our heart is total goodness. Is this blind stupidity or just wishful thinking? I question the depth and breadth of human intelligence, based on this fact alone. Maybe it is just too frightening to face the truth, to take a really close look at what we are.

Religion focuses on good and evil and recognizes the split personality that lies within humankind. Unfortunately, theologians have no answers or spiritual insights about why this dualism exists other than the simple, superficial, God-versus-the-devil explanation. Religion's only antidote for our good/bad impulses is rules to live by. I have learned from my own experience that it is impossible to be good all the time; I would behave well only when it suited me or when I was in the mood. The moral and ethical rules I had been taught meant nothing when my sexual and violent natures came to the surface. Psychologically, we are like angels and creatures from hell rolled into one. It certainly makes life interesting, if nothing else.

I grew up on a cattle ranch in eastern Washington state. Herding livestock is a frustrating experience. On a cattle drive, I and the other ranchers were faced with 250 cows all ambling off in random directions while we tried to herd them in a particular direction. On roundups, we turned into raging beasts. For hours we swore, cussed, kicked the hell out of our horses, and worse. Up in the mountains where nobody else was around to see, we could really be ourselves.

I think it frightened my dad to see me like this, and it certainly scared me to see him in these protracted fits of fury. I guess in the back of my mind I worried that he might turn this uncontrolled force loose on me. It was a good thing we did not pack guns; otherwise we might have killed one of the cows, or maybe one another. As I remember now how captivating it felt to be enveloped by a state of pure, intense rage, I realize I would have gladly and wantonly killed everything and everybody with great pleasure.

Fortunately, I had a small, inquiring, calculating voice inside my head that analyzed the situation and helped me abide by the rules of civilization. This voice was my conscience.

The conscience asks, *Should I do this? Should I do that? Is this right or wrong, good or bad, within the law or outside it? What repercussions are there if I break the rules?* The conscience is completely self-centered, and its motivating force is fear. When the conscience prescribes behavior according to a set of ideals or rules, it has nothing but our own personal interest in mind. It is our survival center; its goal is to keep us in good standing with our parents, the law, and God.

If our conscience is based on fear, then perhaps we have something in common with animals. Fortunately, most of us do not have to deal with the harsh realities of animal life—avoiding the slobbering jaws of some predator.

I have watched enough nature programs to understand the law of the jungle. Occasionally I have wondered what it would feel like to have some ferocious carnivore sink its fangs into the nape of my neck and rake its claws down my back. I can see myself quivering, semiconscious, as my bones are crushed and my blood spurts before the life passes out of me completely. This is the reality of eat or be eaten. This is what animals do. This is the law of the jungle and you will see there is practical application of this law to your own life. We are not above the law of "eat or be eaten."

A friend of mine told me about a television program featuring a naturalist who studied chimpanzees in the wild and videotaped their behavior. My friend related the following story: Next to humans, chimpanzees are some of the most intelligent creatures on earth, and interestingly, they have a taste for monkey. The program showed four or five chimps working together to satisfy this appetite. One chimp, out in the open, chased or herded a group of monkeys into an ambush prepared by the other chimpanzees. After the monkeys passed the point of no return, the chimpanzees singled out one of the monkeys and pounced on their prey from out of nowhere.

My friend could hardly believe his eyes. The chimps literally tore the monkey apart, limb from limb, before it had even stopped screaming. The chimpanzees were in a state that was difficult to describe. It was beyond frenzy. I liken it to the same ecstasy one experiences at the peak of an orgasm; but in this case it was at the peak of destruction, literally ripping the life out of another creature and eating it before the blood had stopped flowing through its arteries. The violence they perpetrated was worse than anything my friend had seen by lions or tigers. It scared me just listening to his story. Thank God I'm not a monkey! I always pictured chimps as docile, playful, cuddly, timid, and fearful little creatures. Vividly exposed, another personality lies hidden behind all the cuteness.

Fear motivates prey to avoid ending up in a predator's jaws. If it weren't for fear and terror, there would be no impetus to avoid this ghastly experience. We humans are similarly inspired by fear to preserve our life and well-being.

Guilt and shame are two varieties of fear: the fear of being exposed for our deeds, the fear of being found out, the fear of being caught or punished, the fear of losing another's grace or our own self-esteem. Guilt is nothing more than the fear of having committed a breach of conduct—of not doing enough for our children, our spouse, or our parents. Shame is the horrible feeling we have, recognizing some deep, irreparable flaw in ourselves.

The superego, one of Freud's three divisions of the psyche, casts a parental eye over our behavior in light of the rules of society and its moral commandments. The superego is where we make decisions about what to do or not to do, then rewards or punishes us through a system of attitudes, conscience, and guilt. God is there, too, looking over our shoulder, also ready to punish or reward depending on our choices. This is how religion, God, the conscience, guilt, and shame are all tied together into one neat package—fear.

Parents teach their children how to behave: An ideal little lady is quiet, shares her toys, and does not talk back. A perfect little gentleman is nonviolent and devoid of malice, hatred, or meanness. Children are told that perfect behavior should be preceded by a perfect heart; anything short of a heart of gold is a defect in our nature, and we should feel ashamed of ourselves for it. Whenever parents harshly reprimand their children for being who they are, that message comes through loud and clear. What we are taught is perceived as the truth, but it is not. We are taught to loathe anything short of perfection in others and especially in ourselves. As a consequence, we become a sort of twisted freak of self-misunderstanding.

More than anyone else, but through no fault of our own, parents are the main instrument of their children's demise. To their children, parents are both nurturing and punishing, encouraging and defeating, loving and hateful, compassionate and castrating. They immerse their children in a sea of love and hate as they praise and chastise with equal force. They build them up, then shatter them.

Religion also demands an idealism in behavior that is impossible to achieve. All children are reminded of their imperfection and, although rarely spoken outright, of their evil. You are a sinner by nature—this is religion's mighty message, which impacts each new generation so strongly that it can lead to a life filled with self-deprecation and hatred, guilt and shame. You do not have to be exposed to formal religious upbringing to be affected. This dogma penetrates all humankind and its institutions.

Religion has both positive and negative aspects. On the one hand, it attempts to teach children love, respect, charity, compassion, and forgiveness. It is a force that is uplifting to all. It supports the weak, the young, and the ill.

On the other hand, religion has powerful negative aspects that contradict the positive force. Most people are aware of the devastating wars that have been fought in the name of religion around the world—many of them still going on today. But even more violent than war is the insidious demand of conditional love and its impossible ideals of behavior set forth by the church and echoed by parents the world round. Children learn at an early age that the love and acceptance of their parents depends on rigid adherence to the unwritten rules set up by centuries of religious tradition and social conditioning. The destructive force of conditional love exists within each of us, stating loud and clear: "If you do what I say, if you believe what I say, if you tow the line, I will love you. If not, I will punish you, reject you, and hate you." This rigid demand seems to leave no room for error, yet the ideal is impossible to live up to.

As a consequence of this sort of upbringing and socialization, we all are preachers of a sort. We conveniently carry around in our mind a rule book for life. As preachers with a self-righteous, holier-than-thou attitude, we hold those around us, especially our children, accountable for their behavior. If they do not measure up, we clobber them.

Our little rule book means everything to us. With it we define friendships, love, loyalty, and goodness. When people fail to live up to our personal standards, we let them know. Perfection is what we expect, and when it is not delivered, we act as judge, jury, and executioner. It is a convenient outlet for being who we are.

Being a moralist allows us infinite leeway to become the supreme praiser or the chief annihilator. We can always find a way to blame our problems on another person's shortcomings. The self-righteous enjoy the ultimate disguise. As we take aim toward others, we are perpetually involved in a never-ending, finger-pointing frenzy of condemnation. In the next minute, either literally or figuratively, we are in bed with them. This is the nature of being human, and more specifically the nature of being conscious. All of us behave the same way. Each of us praises and condemns, builds up or shatters.

Our father and mother have great influence in our life. They play a significant role in teaching us right from wrong and perform the basic process of socializing and civilizing their offspring. Because we are small children for so many years, our father and mother take on larger-than-life proportions. We never rise above their almighty, symbolic giving or punishing hand.

When these concepts are combined, you have the wretched life story of human beings: a fear-crazed, innately sinful, flawed creature quaking under the harsh glare of the judgmental, symbolic parent. Poor, terror-ridden Homo Sapiens in a losing situation tormented by misconception, misunderstanding, missed meaning, and, worst of all, a shattered self-esteem. Nobody wins.

So what is the antidote? Psychoanalysis? Doubtful. The antidote is knowledge. All we can do is blame this whole tragedy on ignorance.

Why can't we see ourselves for what we really are? We are not misshapen, twisted freaks of nature. Quite the contrary. We only seem to be because we do not see ourselves for what we really are.

To know what it is to be human is to become acquainted with a psyche that moves our muscle and bone and orchestrates our life. It loves and hates, builds up and tears down, creates and destroys. On top of that, it is easily frightened, panic-stricken, and terrified. To be conscious is to be something quite extraordinary.

There is so much more to our mental makeup than mere intelligence. Our intelligence has stolen the show, but it plays a bit part in a saga that is infinitely bigger. Intelligence is nothing compared to consciousness. Modern humans have absolutely no idea what it means to be conscious and how that defines who and what we are.

The secrets archaeologists are uncovering about the Mayans help make my point. The Mayans were great astronomers, talented engineers, and builders of majestic cities. But they were also bloodletting destroyers. Their hieroglyphics clearly demonstrate a bloodthirsty bent. Human sacrifice was the essence of their cultural ritual. Their slaughter of human life was in the name of religion, amusement, and economic gain. For entertainment, they would tie a slave into a tight ball and roll him down the side of a pyramid, just to see how high he would bounce.

And yet by no means were the Mayans primitive barbarians. They were modern human beings who lived in highly advanced, civilized settlements, populated by the same sophisticated professions that exist today: rulers, politicians, city planners, architects, engineers, workers, and military personnel. Except for their cultural beliefs and dress, they were the same human beings we are today. Interestingly, we who comprise contemporary affluent societies would like to believe that bloodletting impulses hardly exist today, let alone play any role in our daily life. Today, although distanced from human slaughter, we enjoy it mentally and emotionally by immersing ourselves in it through books, television, and movies.

Something or someone inside our conscious being demands and thrives on love as much as it does on hate and destruction. Something mischievous and playful is going on, and we have no idea who is responsible. And whatever or whoever it is, it influences every aspect of our life. Freud used terms such as instinct, aggressive urges, and sexual lust to describe this heretofore unknown and undefinable thing. Modern scientists and biologists would have us believe that this type of behavior is merely a biological imperative. This is totally absurd. The truth is, no one has the faintest idea what really rests in the conscious. Whatever or whoever it is, it is much bigger than any specific cultural, social, or religious influence on our lives. Twentieth-century American, sixth-century Mayan, or chimpanzee…it makes no difference. What rests in the conscious rules our lives and unalterably defines our true personality.

All the complex emotions and feelings of human beings are composed of three impulses: love, hate, and fear. These three fuels propel us through life. Finding a mate; making love; rearing a child; getting an education; going to work; desiring to live; interacting among friends or enemies, neighbors, lovers, and children; declaring war on our fellow human beings; slaughtering the world with one hand and rebuilding it with the other—all of this is nothing more than a dazed response to the drumbeat of something or someone we do not even know exists, something that pours forth from the fluid of consciousness.

By now you should have a genuine understanding of the human predicament—mistaken identity. Our entire psychological, sociological, and theological understanding of ourselves is built out of half-truths. Our whole existence is a fantasy created by a mind that sees only part of the picture. We are as filled today with ignorance, fear, and superstition as cave dwellers were thousands of years ago.

The truth lies in the nature of consciousness itself. The theory of divinity outlined in the next two chapters provides a better picture of what we are and who we are: Consciousness beings!

Chapter Four

The Theory of Divinity
(Part One)

WHO IS GOD? WHAT IS HIS COMPOSITION? HOW CAN WE DESCRIBE this incomprehensible Being that gives rise to a whole collection of universes? Fortunately, the intellect contained within flesh and blood is capable of understanding. If this were not so, we would be stuck in this mess with no solution. Of course this was not intended to be.

By now it should be obvious that the nature of our true personality is mischievous, playful, and the creator of a game like no other. Only God could develop a game such as this. Only God could create the universe and then throw Himself into it, limited, seemingly vulnerable, and unknowing of who He is. But how is this possible? Is there some better way to understand this divine secret of mistaken identity?

CREATOR, PROTECTOR, DESTROYER

Who is this God? How can He be described? God in His state of undifferentiated singularity is pure Superconsciousness and energy. It is difficult to comprehend anything that is not in some way contained—for example, the way we are contained in our own body. But God in His supreme state of being is not contained; He is beyond time, space, and matter. This divine Consciousness has no boundaries or limitations; He just is! He is pure consciousness and energy; undividable, immutable, and unchangeable. In this state of Superconsciousness, God also has absolute freedom; what He wills becomes. This is what makes God God: the absolute freedom to manifest, to create. What is manifest in this process of manifestation is nothing other than God Himself—it is His own Consciousness that takes on shape and form. He is what becomes manifest, it is He that takes on shape and form in the realm of space and time—which is also His manifestation. Not only does God create the universe out of His own Self, but He also becomes the collection of living beings that fills it (you, me, everything). It is God's will to exist in this way that is the outpouring of the reality we, as limited beings, know. This is His desire: to become the manifest universe. With the absolute freedom of His will and out of His state of Superconsciousness and energy, he becomes.

According to Kashmir Shaivism, this divine consciousness is the essence of Being (the unmanifest state of the divine) and also that of becoming (the manifest state of the divine, the universe). In other words, that which becomes manifest is itself nothing other than pure consciousness; the phenomenal world of matter, shape, and form is simply consciousness congealed or contracted. We as individual human beings are literally contracted clumps of God's consciousness. Therefore it is this God of consciousness that is the nature of all things. There is only Consciousness and nothing else. Nothing exists that is not Consciousness. It is either free and unbound or clumped. Once this Divine Consciousness becomes contracted or congealed, it loses its omnipotence; it takes on worldly characteristics and loses its sense of fullness.

Most important to our understanding of God's play is that He limits His own Self so that He becomes contracted, limited, and essentially powerless. This is who you and I are, Lord Siva (pronounced "Shiva," another name for God, or the universal self, as used in Kashmir Shaivism), in His contracted state of limitation. In this state of limited being there is no longer an awareness of our super state of being; there is no longer an experience of fullness, completeness, or absolute freedom—the true nature of His Consciousness. Instead of experiencing the entire universe as an expansion of our self, we have taken on individuality. This self-imposed limitation is the veil of ignorance that keeps Him from recognizing His own self.

But we as limited individual human beings are conscious, and this consciousness that we possess is the same as divine consciousness, although now constricted and imperfect (it is no longer aware of the totality of its own state, unbound and unlimited). Instead of seeing the universe as part of our self, we now see our self as a part of the universe.

It is the nature of consciousness to be aware, to be perceptive. And of what is this consciousness aware? Who or what does it perceive? It perceives its own self. Most incredible is the realization that this consciousness is not only the perceiver but also the manifested object of perception. If, as mentioned above, the world is nothing but congealed consciousness, consciousness not only contains the act of perception, but also manifests itself externally as its own perceived object. In other words, there is only consciousness; out of this comes both the observer and that which is observed. For Lord Siva in His unlimited state of being, the perception is "I am That." For the limited being, the world is perceived as being completely separate from himself or herself. For God, the object contained within His consciousness is experienced as part of Himself, His own expansion; there is no difference between that object and Himself. For the limited being, the object of his or her perception (earth, trees, stars, the moon, the sun, other people, animals) appears separate from his or her own self.

In the unlimited state of being, the subject (God) and object (His Creation), the perceiver and the perceived, are undividedly one. Here the universe remains undifferentiated where the "I" and "That" are the same thing. In the limited state of being, by a trick only God could perform, the perceiver and that which is perceived differentiate; they seem to split apart and become separate from one another. As the universe unfolds or coagulates in the process of manifestation, the observer and the object of perception split and the observer feels separate from that which surrounds him or her. Instead of perceiving the universe as one undivided mass of divine consciousness, the limited perceiver sees it as a collection of individual objects that are separate from his or her own self.

In the final analysis, this whole thing is a trick and nothing more. God is God and never anything but God. Even in our state of limitation, we are God—though we do not know it. Simply put, we exist in two states of being, both equally valid, each part of the other. Both states exist simultaneously, each giving rise to the other. As God contracts Himself into a state of limitation, the expansion of the universe rises in His awareness as perceived by the limited being. As God withdraws His awareness from the universe, He returns to that state of the Absolute, above and beyond time, space, and limitation; the abode of Lord Siva. These are the internal and external aspects of the same God, the same one Being, the Existent One.

The Theory of Divinity (Part One)

This is the play of Divine Consciousness. From within the substance of its own self arises the manifest universe.

Those who have attained self-realization become Lord Siva even while existing in a body, and can freely rise to their undifferentiated state of superconscious Being or lower themselves into their state of differentiated awareness. By their free will they can go up or down, however they please. This we cannot do! We have come down but cannot rise.

The secret of all secrets is that the individual, limited self is identical to the universal Self, Lord Siva. The very nature of Lord Siva is to manifest Himself externally, to make visible His incredible creative nature. God makes the collection of ideas that are internally contained within His own consciousness come to life as the visible universe. Unlike our own ideas, God's actually come to life, they become real—they take on shape and form. This is His power.

Now in His play, God in His limited state of Being is filled with these questions: *Who am I? What am I?* These questions haunt those of the human race.

Incredible as it seems, all the manifestations, all the superdrama that unfolds in our life is nothing other than the creative ideations of Lord Siva Himself. But now, trapped in this state, lost, forgetful of who He is and the victim of a never-ending set of circumstances that demonstrate the magnitude of His vulnerability, His freedom and power almost extinguished, His consciousness so constricted as to give an imperfect impression of reality, totally ignorant, this God of the universe is now the fool in a fool's drama. What are we to do?

What are we to do but try and comprehend? The ultimate questions are *How can I know my own self?* and *Where is the secret revealed that shows me who I really am?* The answer to this question is contained in the next chapter.

45

Chapter Five

The Theory of Divinity
(Part Two)

WE NEED TO TAKE THE THEORY OF KASHMIR SHAIVISM ONE STEP further. In this game, Lord Siva creates the universe out of His own Consciousness and then, by a process only He could perform, loses Himself in it. Only Siva would have the power to bind himself, limit himself, constrict himself, and forget himself. This process is a progressive coagulation of consciousness whereby God's awareness of His totality becomes more and more constricted and fragmented. This arc of descent is built out of the thirty-six tattvas (elements), bottoming out in gross matter such as rock. This ladder of descent, the stepwise, progressive coagulation of His consciousness ending in the materialization of the gross elements, leads to the world we know. This ladder also leads back to our throne.

The thirty-six tattvas describe the process by which God descends into the world of limitation and also the process of His ascent. At the very top, there exists only "I." Then comes an increasing vividness of "I am That" (the universe). The first five tattvas, starting from Lord Siva's Supreme State of Being and working downward, describe the progressively increasing vividness of the manifest universe in His awareness. Even at the level of the fifth tattva, the experience of Lord Siva is still such that He and the universe are one and the same ("This am I"). As Lord Siva continues to climb down this ladder of His own making, He becomes lost and forgetful of who He is. From now on He does not know that He is Lord Siva.

From this point down Lord Siva moves from the realm of the infinite that is beyond space and time into the realm of the finite, into a universe that is measurable: Maya, the level of the sixth tattva. Here is the beginning of individuality. Going further downward through another five tattvas, Lord Siva further binds and limits Himself so that He completely loses His omnipotence. Now He is very close to the realm of humanity, lost, totally unknowing of His true nature, and powerless.

At the level of the twelfth tattva, Lord Siva exists as Purusa. Purusa is aware but powerless. This is pure subjective awareness, God Consciousness, albeit constricted and limited at this stage. Intimately connected to Purusa is his power, Prakriti (the thirteenth tattva). Prakriti has no awareness but is the primal matter or ground (power) by which its undifferentiated potential gives rise to the objective world through a succession of additional tattvas, namely the cognitive function contained within our own head that projects the objective world on its screen. In other words, the successive differentiation or manifestation of the world occurs right inside our own brain such that the world we perceive—rocks, trees, buildings, people, animals, everything, and everybody—takes on shape and form inside our own heads and is experienced as separate from our own self. This is how Lord Siva exists in humans.

This is a journey downward that each and all of us take as Lord Siva becomes the entire multitude of limited subjects. Regardless of our limitation, however, underneath all of this worldly ignorance is our true Self; in the final analysis we are God and never anything but God; this is what we have to come to understand. There is much to learn and much to do, but part of the process of self-discovery is the process of self-recognition, to try and remember, comprehend, and conceptualize what we really are: Lord Siva.

This doctrine of recognition is called Pratyabhijna. It is a process of trying to see ourselves for what we are even in this worldly state of limited being. We have to stretch our imagination, to open to new ideas. This process of recognition starts with a mental picture, a new way of thinking about ourselves. Even though the innermost reality of who we are seems distant, there is a hint of Lord Siva that shines brightly in the realm of mortal beings—this hint of Lord Siva is His Fivefold Acts. We can know that we are in fact Lord Siva because, like him, we also perform these acts. In our limited state of being they are called actions. Lord Siva creates, protects and maintains, destroys, conceals Himself, and reveals Himself. Because we are Lord Siva, we also (in a very limited way) do the same.

Lord Siva has the power to create, protect what He has created, and destroy what He has created. That is what He does, that is who He is: the Creator/Protector/Destroyer. God is the ultimate Creator/Protector/Destroyer; this is the very nature of Divine Consciousness. But Consciousness also possesses this inherent force and direction in the limited state of individual being—to be conscious is to be the creator/protector/destroyer. Even though Consciousness is in Its self-imposed state of limitation, contraction, and fragmentation, Its essence—that of the creator, protector, and destroyer—prevails. This is who we are as individual beings, and it is this trace of Lord Siva that prevails even in His limited state of being.

We are this creator, protector, destroyer. We do not understand this basic composition that is the quintessence of who we are and that causes us to behave the way we do. This is our downfall. But in this adventure of self-discovery, one has to know and be in control. This is a must. To unravel the mystery of life is in part to come to grips with this inherent nature of Consciousness and then be its master. In Lord Siva's state of contraction and forgetfulness (which is our state of contraction and forgetfulness), we no longer remember our nature, nor do we feel connected to that which surrounds us. Therefore we act inappropriately. We become base and crude, angry and violent. We neither know who we are nor recognize what surrounds us as part of our own self. Consequently, we build our world with one hand and destroy it with the other.

In the remainder of this book, you will learn more about the limited creator/protector/destroyer and the havoc it creates. To understand, then take control—that is the first step, the challenge.

At least by now you are getting an idea of who you are! For me, this idea grows day by day.

Chapter Six

The True Nature of Consciousness

WE HUMANS, ALTHOUGH BLESSED WITH SELF-AWARENESS AND INTEL-lectual skills, are nonetheless a part of nature and its grand design. The fact that we are conscious beings defines our nature. This nature pulsates within us. We are both the beneficiaries and the victims of its forces.

We humans exude creativity. The outward manifestation of this force rests behind all our desires and all that we do. We yearn to create new life, make families, and provide our loved ones with a home. We are great builders of communities, cities, and nations. We are constantly creating new science and technology, fine artwork and great literature. In our own special way, we are consumed by this creative force. It is behind everything that comes into being, from the evening meal to business deals, from backyard landscaping to skyscrapers. To exist is to have been created.

CREATOR, PROTECTOR, DESTROYER

We also exude destructiveness—a force that rests behind our deepest desires and the things we do. It shatters all we have worked so hard to build: love, marriage, family, home, career, peace on earth. Whatever exists, from cherished moral principles, to the streets of the world, to human life, we destroy it all with vigor and zest. In each and every one of us, our blood boils with destructive force and anger.

Sometimes I think God threw me to the bottom of the barrel, but left me with a flicker of self-awareness so that I would eventually become painfully aware of my total lack of refinement and my destructiveness—the creator, protector, and destroyer run amok. The essence of humanity is captured in my own being.

How are these all-encompassing, almost incomprehensible forces expressed in our emotional nature? As love and hate. Our personal lives are a saga of these forces. We live in a sea of love and hate. Even under the best circumstances and the tightest control, they push their way through the cracks in our facade. Life is a chaotic mess because of this strange mix of passionate opposites. Not to understand the creative and destructive and who and what they represent is to lead a life filled with pain and suffering.

This reality can be understood esoterically as a never-ending pulsation of creation and destruction that manifests as the known universe. This rhythm, this vibration, this pulsation of creation and destruction comes forth from the center of a bigger reality, of which our senses have no awareness and knowledge, no understanding. By a trick that only the greatest of sages understand, the infinite power of this creative and destructive force that brings forth this whole existence is downscaled, reduced, and brought into the finite as it manifests itself in our own being. This book offers a glimpse of that span between infinite power and finite power, from the immeasurable to the measurable, from infinite knowledge to the finite known. This story is about creation, protection, and destruction and the Creator/Protector/Destroyer. From an emotional and psychological point of view, love and hate are our outward manifestations of the ubiquitous forces of creation and destruction that fill each and all of us, the very essence of consciousness itself. Therefore, our real personality is not one but two. One half can only love. The other can only hate. Both are operating every second, on top of every issue, moving us one way or the other. Our basic psychological makeup is more powerful than our good intentions. The strength of what and who we are is stronger than the power of civilized thought. Morality crumbles at the feet of this unknown personality. With these powerful forces we are building up, protecting, nurturing with one side, and destroying everything and everyone with the other. Our makeup causes us to be this way.

Because of this, we humans are living, walking, talking contradictions, and life becomes a never-ending parade of inconsistencies. We cause as much hurt and misery as we do joy and happiness. We repeat the same offenses against those we love, but there is no learning from our mistakes. For unknown reasons, we do and say things that seem beyond our control, or say one thing, then do another. Intellectually we plan a course that is straight and true, but instead we zigzag between good and bad, love and hate. We teach and preach ideal behavior to our children but can never set the example. Our words are empty; our actions speak for themselves.

Why? The reason does not exist in the realm of purposeful decision making. There is no absolute right or wrong, good or bad. It is pointless to try to comprehend this in a religious framework. The reason rests in what and who we are. We cut a wide swath—at home, at work, with our kids— and none of it is on purpose. You cannot blame yourself any more than you can hold a rabbit or a pig or a wolf responsible for its behavior. What do they know? Nothing. What do we know? Nothing. That is, until now.

Most people believe we are already well on our way to conquering nature; this, however, is absurd. Human ingenuity has accomplished some fantastic feats. No one could dispute that we have harnessed nature and invented some wonderful devices to benefit all humanity. We have also brought new meaning to the words weapon and destruction. But we have conquered nothing.

That is why our words, actions, and behavior seem absurd and unthinkable half the time. We are ashamed of ourselves as often as we are self-congratulatory. This inconsistency permeates every aspect of our life and does not change as we mature. We are constantly repairing and rebuilding what we destroy—our family, our business, and especially our-selves. Even those things that we want most of all—lasting, meaningful relationships and happiness for our children—crumble before our eyes. The reason is that all three of our personalities are involved in everything we do. No wonder there is confusion of the mind and pain and suffering; life could not be anything but a tragedy!

Not understanding the nature of who we are—that is, conscious beings—makes life difficult, puzzling, and at times intolerably painful. Psychological theorists try to offer answers or comfort, but none is avail-able. Most people believe that they are the only ones stymied by and suf-fering from their inconsistent behavior, but that is not true. These three personalities—creator/protector/destroyer—rest in every person; all humankind suffers from mistaken identity.

On the other hand, you should not become filled with despair. I have learned above all else that the potential for joy and happiness exists. The key is working with, not against, our inborn makeup.

The True Nature of Consciousness

Somehow I always missed recognizing half my identity, even though both parts exist in equal strength and affect my behavior to the same degree. Although most humans see the good in themselves, they have a great deal of difficulty recognizing their darker side. Ignorant and naive, we have assumed that all of our motives come from good intentions—I certainly did. Nonetheless, we are split right down the middle. The destroyer is in plain sight, but we have not seen it because it is subtly camouflaged by the creator.

Good deeds are intertwined with bad. The bad is intertwined with good. Love is intertwined with hate. Hate is intertwined with love. Overt or subtle, nobody seems to see what is going on inside one's own self. We are kind and content, uplifting and compassionate one minute, angry and depressed the next. We can cry because something touches our hearts, and ten seconds later, we turn into someone vicious and cruel. We unleash these forces on one another with a fury that has no mercy. The wheel keeps on turning. Good…bad…good…bad—love…hate…love…hate. You might like to think there is more to it than this—some lofty psychological complexity to ponder—but this is our true profile. It is not a flaw of nature; it is nature, it is the nature of consciousness itself. In fifteen minutes of family interaction on a Saturday afternoon these personalities will emerge and reemerge innumerable times.

The destructive half of our personality demands a never-ending supply of victims, and we take them all day long. Half the satisfaction we derive from life is in destroying others. We love to do this. We enjoy nothing more than tearing somebody apart during dinner conversation; it is with exactly the same passion that a tiger twists the flesh of an antelope. Nothing is more exciting than learning of another's misfortune or demise.

The destructive force is the essence of annihilation. It is absolute, pure hatred and disdain for everything and everyone. We are filled with these emotions all day long, even though we are usually not aware of them. One force gives rise to anger, meanness, negativity, and brutality, not to mention overt physical violence. Whatever exists, we destroy—love, marriage, children, friendship, promises—even our own selves. Then our other core being expresses love, warmth, and goodness.

All people are the same. Wealth, breeding, nobility, even royalty mean absolutely nothing. No facade of sophistication, no degree of religious training or education will have the slightest impact on the structure of our makeup. We all make and break promises and commitments. We build trust, then destroy it with the same incredible energy. This is the story of human interaction. These personalities do as they please—or should I say, they do as they please as long as they are unseen and unrecognized, camouflaged in ignorance and superstition.

By now, for the first time, I have some sort of understanding. We are what we are, and that's all there is to it. These opposites operate under one skin, inside one head. The creative/destructive impulse within us not only equates to love and hate, but also to its more primitive manifestations: sex and violence. The outward flow of these energies polarizes our body and mind as we interact with others. This is what life is about. Sex and love on one hand and rage and destruction on the other.

Every child witnesses these two personalities growing up. Growing up can be as painful as it can be pleasurable and fun. We grow up in an environment of love and hate, good and bad. Most enjoy tremendous nurturing and positivity in their homes, but there is always an equal amount of anger and negativity. No doubt family members love one another, but we are all simultaneously filled with a darker side. It is safe to say when it comes to family, our shortcomings seem equal to our love and warmth. The things we do to each other are beyond description, especially to the ones we love.

Do parents know their psychological makeup? How could they have known? Nobody knows the truth.

As I was growing up, I was equally filled with good and bad. I was loving and warm, the protector and big brother to my younger sister. At other times I was so mean and cruel that thinking about it now, many years later, sends shivers up my spine. It is surprising that we all manage as well as we do. One thing is for certain: We are all survivors.

The creator/protector/destroyer motivates us, moves us, and compels us to do what we do. These are the same forces that compel animals to do what they do. But do not let that mislead you into thinking that our primitive urges and violent nature might be a vestigial remnant from some crude evolutionary ancestor. By now you know this is not the case. What I am talking about is bigger than the biggest. Our heritage is much grander and much older than lizards. Our lineage goes back to the beginning, long before there was any life at all.

Chapter Seven

Monism

How can we possibly trace from whence we came? Where do our roots lie? What existed before life?

In the beginning there was neither naught nor aught:
Then there was neither sky nor atmosphere above.
Then there was neither day nor night nor light nor darkness,
Only the Existent One breathed calmly, self-contained.
                                    —Ancient Sanskrit Chant

To the wise, the spark of energy within all life is part of something billions of times bigger than anything we can know or see, something that supports the whole reality. From this state of pure energy comes an infinite variety of life, shape, and form: the whole universe and all of its individual parts. Synonymous with this state of pure energy is pure consciousness, and from within this comes creation and destruction; that is, the creator/destroyer.

Being part of something so basic, so universal, means that we are not separate from the rest of the universe; we are interconnected and the same. The same creator/destroyer is in all things, from a butterfly to a human being. Think about a butterfly. It has absolutely no idea why it exists, where it came from, or how it survives and makes new life. But it all happens quite successfully because a universal intelligence pervades all things. This Super Being inside gives it life, directs and maintains its life, and then absorbs its life back into the universal womb from which it came. Humans are no different; we have within us an Infinite Wisdom that orchestrates the overall theme of our life. We do have a will of our own, but it is small and weak compared to Its will. This great power causes our cells to divide and our heart to beat. Every movement, every thought, every breath, every feeling and emotion is powered by this Super Being. What we feel, think, and do is what It thinks, feels, and does.

The fact is that we are Lord Siva, even now, but as long as we identify with our limited state of being and not our universal state of being, we remain limited, vulnerable, and dependent. Only in our state of universal being are we totally independent and free. Limited, we are caught in a never-ending set of circumstances we cannot control.

Most of us believe that we are the master of our own destiny. But this is absurd. The overall theme of our lives rests with Lord Siva; He creates the circumstances that engulf us each step of the way in our own personal life. On the other hand, we do have some control over our lives, and this is where the challenge begins. We have the capacity to choose—to choose whether to be good or bad as each of these circumstances in our lives presents itself. We have the choice to act with a gentle compassion and understanding or destroy everything in our path. We are creator/destroyers, and this causes us to be the way we are. What could be more interesting or more challenging?

The quality I am talking about goes far beyond ordinary morality and ethical behavior. My goal is to develop a gentleness for the world and the people who fill it—the same gentleness a parent has for a newborn child; to develop a compassion for humankind as big as the ocean.

What this means to me is that all of life is a challenge, every single minute of the day. Running away to the isolated wilderness accomplishes nothing. A life filled with renunciation and austerity accomplishes nothing. The challenge associated with Kashmir Shaivism is to conquer one's nature, not try and escape it.

Once I understood my true composition, I could do something about it. I was obligated to live more consciously than I ever had before, to develop the strength of my will. I had to take more responsibility for my actions—much more. From that point forward, good action is what I was after. This is the price and the reward of this great knowledge, taking responsibility. Instead of being a puppet on a string or stage prop in a drama we do not even know exists, it is time to ask *What am I?* and *Who am I?*—and then try and comprehend. It is at this point that we can begin to break out of our limited state of being.

Most people are taught from childhood that the universe is divided. Christianity and Islam purport that there are good and evil, God against the devil, that which is divine and that which is not. God stands on one side of the line, and everything else is on the other. This dualistic philosophy implies that there is force and substance in the universe that is not God's. The "ungodly," imperfect and flawed, is responsible for chaos, disharmony, destruction, and evil. This belief has the tragic effect of indoctrinating its followers with the idea that the unholy rests within them. These self-debasing, self-hating people are doomed because, from a purely psychological viewpoint, they can never overcome the evil they believe is within them.

Most Eastern spirituality fares no better. Vedantic philosophy recognizes the forces of nature but believes they should be denounced. This philosophy holds that God is real, but all else, including the universe, is an illusion. Love and hate, good and bad, destruction and creation—none of it exists or has any meaning. Because the universe is unreal, it should be rejected and disregarded. It is easy to say that this existence is unreal, but applying that so-called wisdom to a person's daily life is much more difficult. The belief that all existence is an illusion precludes any satisfactory answer to the concerns *Who am I?* and *What am I?*

Is there no philosophy that can soothe humanity's hearts and minds? Our predicament is not the work of the devil, nor is it illusory or unreal. We are real; the universe is real; the chaos is real. When you stop to think about it, Eastern Vedantic spirituality is not much different from Western religion—we all traditionally denounce, hate, and reject what we are. Human beings' only imperfection is their limited ability to perceive the God within them and to experience what it feels like to be God.

A theology has little meaning if it does not work in its application to our daily life. A belief system should be a guide, a blueprint, an inspiration for refinement and empowerment. Most great religions of the world offer rules to live by; what they lack is a message to motivate their followers to go beyond merely trying to live by the rules, but to try and eventually succeed.

Only the truth, the correct philosophic view of God and His connectedness to this universe, will produce the desired result for the individual and for all of humankind. All lesser doctrines would fall short in changing the direction of the world. They do not contain within them the capacity to generate the intensity of inspiration and enthusiasm needed to obtain their goal. Lesser doctrines never solve the riddle of *Who am I?* and *What am I?* Because identity and ethics go hand in hand, each is powerless without the other; there is never any empowerment of the individual.

By the grace of God, there are the teachings of Lakshmanjoo and the supreme philosophy of Kashmir Shaivism, which has the potential to change the world, one person at a time.

Because God is everything, there is nothing that is not God. He is all that is good and all that is evil. He is the springtime. He is the force that makes grass grow, the warmth of the sun that renews. He is the bud, the blossom, and new birth. He is also cold and illness. He is the rampant destruction of natural disasters. He is the might responsible for pestilence, filth, and all that which would seem perversely unmentionable.

God is the freshness of a flower and the beauty in a child. He is the murderer and the racist. In church it is God who is singing in the choir, giving the sermon, and sitting in the pews below. At home and behind closed doors, it is God who is the spouse abuser, rapist, and child molester. Behind these same doors, it is God who gives love, warmth, and affection. God is starvation, drought, and deadly viruses. God is the pope and the president, the thief and the whore. It is all the Almighty's drama. He is this spark that brings flesh and blood to life. Life is made out of His being.

In Europe it was God who tortured and slaughtered the Jews in every conceivable way. In Nuremberg it was God who sat as judge, jury, and executioner for those who carried out heinous wartime crimes. In Rwanda, Israel, Bangladesh, Somalia, Bosnia-Herzegovina (to name only a few corners of the world), God is the perpetrator of a never-ending bloodbath frenzy.

In God's state of supreme being, this whole reality manifests out of His own self. He becomes what He creates. When some incomprehensible tragedy occurs, where hundreds or even thousands of innocent people are slaughtered, most people cannot believe that God had anything to do with it. According to monism, God had everything to do with it. What actually happens depends on a person's perspective. From God's perspective in His supreme state of being, nothing has happened at all but play. The whole event was divine play. Nothing was lost, nothing gained. God played all the roles, including the victim and the victimizer. He experienced no pain or suffering; all the drama is just the transformation of divine Consciousness into one form or another.

On the other hand, from our perspective as ignorant, limited, individual beings, it is hard to see divinity in these acts; we see only evil. In God's supreme state of being, all acts are divine. In our state of being, we are accountable for our actions and there is good and evil.

What this means is that this worldly drama is perceived from two different perspectives. One perspective is from God's unlimited state. The other perspective is from God's limited state (our perspective), the realm of good and evil. This is His game and how He plays it. This is why He created this limited perspective in the first place, for the intrigue.

At one level there is only play. At the other level there is pain, suffering, absolute torture, a tormented existence where there seems no relief in any corner. Only God could come up with a scheme such as this. How very mischievous. And how difficult it is to remember that God is simultaneously playing both of these perspectives. In fact, God plays every role, from one extreme to the other.

What this means is there is a challenge; there is work to be done. Even though limited, we possess a will and have a choice in our actions and behavior. What this means is that we as limited beings have no control over the circumstances that befall us. These circumstances belong to the unlimited Being, Lord Siva. But we do play a part in that we have a choice: As each circumstance presents itself, we choose how we are going to react. Those who are wise read between the lines in order to see what is happening in their life. In other words, God creates the setting and we make the final brush stroke in the drama of life. We have this choice. If we do it right, we move on. If we do not do it right, the same circumstances will repeat themselves one lifetime into the next until we do get it right, then we move onto something new. This is an interesting high-stakes game that keeps going on and on—until you win.

Of the utmost importance, and the key to understanding spirituality (God) and how to make this philosophy work, is the concept of will. Only God has a free will. We do not. Our action is dependent on the will of God. God can do anything He pleases, creative or destructive. After all, whatever God does is a game unto His own self; furthermore, God does not do good or bad action; all of God's acts are divine. But as for us, in our ignorance and limitation, unrealized and unappreciative of our true identity, we do good and bad actions. Developing the strength of our will is the pathway to power and divinity. This is the knowledge of the Supreme Secret. The first step is to realize that God can do whatever He wants; we cannot, not as limited individual beings. The key is to move from grossness and irresponsibility to refinement and total responsibility for all of our actions—big and small. Making all our actions into good actions is the essence of this philosophical practice for beginners. Each and every day I wake up means another chance to get it right.

The Supreme Being is the creator/destroyer in all things. Time would not exist; motion, space, and shape would not be; nothing could exist except for God's presence and desire. By His will alone and out of His own consciousness and energy, God creates, supports, and destroys all that exists.

We are intimately involved in this grand scheme of creation and destruction by moving in and out of states of nothingness and existence. According to Lakshmanjoo, two states of being exist in the universe, at opposite ends of the spectrum. One state is like nothingness. It is dimensionless, formless, timeless, and motionless. Nothingness is one indivisible state of being. Here no opposites exist—only consciousness, energy, and potential. It is from this homogenous state of Consciousness that whatever God desires—including you and me—will arise, by His free will alone, and move into the dimension of time, form, motion, and change.

The state of differentiation and individuality exists at the other end of the spectrum, represented by the cycle of birth and death. For most Westerners, birth and death have ominous meanings. But birth and death mean only a change, a transition from one state of being to the other and back. Rest assured, there is no such thing as death. The way of the cosmos and all nature is cyclical; life moves toward death, then what seems like death flows toward life. We make the transition from a state of universal undifferentiation to a state where we take on individual shape and form. We spring from nothingness, and we return to nothingness. It is all arranged by one Super Being that rests in all things.

Lakshmanjoo explained that there is a lot more to this reality than most of us can appreciate or know. Atoms and subatomic particles create a background world that we cannot easily see, but we know exists. Something even more subtle precedes atoms and subatomic particles, and our entire reality is comprised of those components.

There are the gross, the subtle, and the subtlest, which give rise to this existence. Each of these three allows for an increasingly differentiated state of manifestation. All we know is the outermost manifestation, the gross. The subtle and the subtlest are accessible only through conscious awareness. Scientific instrumentation and probing cannot penetrate beyond the gross.

Gross reality, which includes atoms, subatomic particles, neutrons, and so on, is made of the subtle. The subtle cannot be perceived by physical means. It is nonexistent through ordinary observation. Nonetheless, this entire reality we know is the outward manifestation of the subtle.

To go even deeper, the subtle is the outward manifestation of the subtlest. Even though it would seem like nothingness from our frame of reference, it is not. The subtlest form of this reality is where this seeming nothingness first starts to transform into differentiated shape. Some alteration has occurred, but as of yet it is undefinable.

The boundary between the subtlest and the subtle exists just at that point where matter, space, and time begin to take on characteristics. The subtle turns into the gross where matter, time, and change become clearly apparent. In the same way that a television signal gives rise to an image on a television screen, whatever the subtle and subtlest are, they give rise to everything.

Those who can exist in this way can change the final shape and form of the gross reality we live in before it even happens. This makes them extremely unique and equally powerful; it makes them God. Lakshman-joo was aware of and moved freely among all three states. This is how he enabled my wife and me to have a daughter after so many years of our being childless. He created Amanda out of His consciousness.

It was interesting to me to learn that there are those who exist in the unlimited state of being while inhabiting a human body, but do not have the power to come down to their limited state of being. They are trapped "up," in the higher state—as most of us are trapped "down," in the limited state. We have the power to come down but not to rise. Those who are trapped in this higher state see everything as divine. To them, opposites do not exist: good and bad, virtuous and evil are the same. They experience all that surrounds them as an outpouring of their own selves. In this state of being, there is nothing to do and nowhere to go. Everything is perfect; therefore, they see no need to change anything in the world. They are complete within themselves. Only someone such as Lakshmanjoo, who had the power to move at will from the unlimited state (up) to the limited state (down), could affect the course of humanity. One must experience the world in order to want to influence it.

The meaning of life for humans at the grossest level is love and hate. We love and hate everybody simultaneously. This gives our existence passion, meaning, and direction. At this level, however, nothing changes, and pain and suffering are constant. It is this passion that keeps us earthbound, that keeps us from ascending that ladder from which we came. One cannot move up this ladder unless we give up this passion. You cannot take it with you.

As we become more refined, we neither love nor hate the individual who is still filled with these emotions. Instead, we love the divinity that rests under the surface. This is the first step in the process of rising.

Although Lakshmanjoo had reached that state of paraBhairava, where Lord Siva exists as the Supreme "I," He chose to remain in His body out of His ocean of compassion for humans' (Lord Siva's) predicament. He was a living example of God's message. It was not so much what he said but how he acted that brought those around Him to their knees. When He did speak, He rarely spoke of anything but God. To Him there was nothing else and that was His message for those who cared to listen. Even though Lakshmanjoo's body passed away in the fall of 1991, surely he exists in the state of seeming nothingness, where he continues to affect all of our lives. By the nature of who He is, He is a part of all of us.

This God of Consciousness is so great that it supersedes time, space, and matter. We live at one end of this intensity of power. It is all we are familiar with—our selves, our families, our jobs, our communities. It is the creator/destroyer at its most gross outwardly manifestation—that is, in fact, you and me. That is what this book is all about, our roughest edges and the sagas God creates in our daily life. But do not despair. From a state that precedes the most subtle all the way to the gross, it is one indivisible being: God. When you look in the mirror from this day on and meet your own eyes, do not look away. You are no longer seeing a flawed, unholy mortal destined to live a life out of control until the day of your death. You are looking at God! Unfortunately, from this perspective, we cannot see what we are—not yet, anyway.

Chapter Eight

A Fool's Drama

How very strange is this life of ours. I am sure most people would admit that they never expected anything like this. We grow up with a set of ideals, a set of expectations about how life should be, but what actually happens to us is something completely different.

Most first encounter this dilemma in early childhood; unfortunately, things only get worse as we get older. Even though parents, teachers, and religious institutions follow a similar blueprint for teaching social, moral, and ethical behavior, life still is a nightmare. Parents tell their children that above all else they want them to be happy and satisfied, to get a good education, to find the right job, to fall in love with the right person, have a family, and live happily ever after. Children listen to their parents and teachers as if to learn this formula for happiness, success in life, and peace of mind. Unfortunately, this is a world filled with fools. We are all fools in a fool's drama. Each new generation of fools teaches the next generation of fools the meaning of life and the pathway to nowhere—to a life of torture.

Please do not take offense at this. You will see there is no reason to become upset once you realize this predicament is bigger than anyone could possibly imagine. There is no blaming here, nor any reason to be ashamed. We are about to embark on the greatest adventure this world has to offer, and we are starting from the bottom. So just read on and try to relax and understand. That is what I am trying to do: I am trying to understand the immensity of Lakshmanjoo's teachings.

Most people spend a lifetime trying to bring order and meaning to their life; invariably, they end in failure. The reason for this is simple: There is no solution to life's predicament in a fool's drama. True success is impossible unless it is the success defined by a fool. For the fool, happiness and joy are impossible to keep; peace of mind comes only fleetingly; living happily ever after is a storybook fantasy—nothing more. There is only one reason for being born; those who ignore this calling are the fools who fill this world.

Human beings spend a lifetime caught in a vicious cycle, vacillating between opposite extremes. We are filled with love one minute and hate the next; first being good and then bad; making up and then breaking up. In this world there is no true refinement or concept of the reality at hand. As there seems to be no escape from this world of opposites, by definition we can only lose. It is a drama that turns life into a downward spiral of perpetual pain and suffering. This is the way of the world for those who do not understand—fools living in a fool's drama. Understandably, this great pain and suffering motivates a desperate search for the truth, but nobody becomes any wiser. Families are shattered, the hearts of children are broken, everything that is important crumbles before our eyes. Events repeat themselves, even though promises for a new beginning are made with equal frequency.

What we are facing becomes relatively simple once it is explained in a way that makes sense. This entire drama of ignorance and foolishness is a trick, a divine trick in which God pulls the wool over His own eyes in an incredible game of hide and seek. He loses Himself in you and me as the fool.

Ultimately, God rediscovers Himself, in spite of His trick. To be a total fool and eventually discover that you are God is His play. What could be more exciting? Being of this world is simply to start the journey upward, nothing more. There is nothing to accomplish here but working toward this end. Of course this is almost impossible to comprehend for those who have never thought about God. Most of us are so entrenched in life—striving for success, getting educated, attempting to make ends meet, looking for love, taking care of our children—where does God fit into the picture?

It is both astounding and humorous to stand back and watch the ridiculous drama of human interaction. This fool's drama is the drama of politics; it is the drama of war and peace; it is the drama of interaction between husband and wife, parent and child. Fools live in the world of opposites, acting out each extreme with equal vigor—calling for peace and harmony out of one corner of their mouth while declaring war out of the other. This is the nature of life for humans: happy one minute, shattered the next. Because we generally have no idea why things are the way they are, nothing really improves over time, even though most of us are desperate for change. With this same drama going on at work, at home—absolutely everywhere—there is no escape or relief from it in any corner, by any ordinary means. There is only one way out.

By definition, the fool will not be convinced easily. By definition, the fool is born to suffer, to live a life of torture; that is, unless we ask those questions *Who am I?* and *What am I?* and then pursue the adventure of self-realization. There is no other reason for this predicament and no other solution to this dilemma. All other theories pertaining to this universal tragedy are written by fools. Who am I for writing such a thing? Someone who believes from the bottom of my heart the words of Lakshmanjoo. Who am I but just another person desperately searching for the truth as to the meaning of life? Who am I but a person who has fallen in love with the words of his master? In the final analysis, spirituality is but a love story.

Even for fools, there is a way out. That is why we are here. This is what makes this game so exciting. Who are these fools, anyway? No one other than the Existent One Himself. There is no reason to take offense when trying to picture yourself as the fool, because you are one. You have to ground yourself in reality to play this game. This is the starting point, the place where you begin to put things in perspective.

I cannot stress to the reader strongly enough the importance of trying to conceptualize what is going on here. These ideas should be exciting, not degrading. This entire drama is a divine game and nothing more. It has no other meaning except play for Lord Siva—He has limited himself by playing the role of the fool only so that, from his perspective, He can rediscover His true nature. What more ridiculous, hilarious, mischievous, lowly position could he assume?

It takes a fair amount of intelligence, not to mention humility, to do this. What else do fools have to hang on to but their ego? Is it not human nature to be in a state of constant self-repair, shoring up and repairing the integrity of our self-esteem? For fools, this is a full-time endeavor. But for those looking for greatness, eventually this puny ego that commands the body, mind, and emotions must go. You must make room for expansion.

The starting point in this grand adventure must be the realm of everyday life. Fools are both victims and victimizers in this saga of pain, suffering, and ignorance. There are two goals in this adventure for beginners: first, to add no further pain and suffering to our own personal world and, second, to repair your own self, that is forgive, forget, and become healthy and strong physically, mentally, and emotionally. We cannot succeed if we are broken down, depressed, or in the final stages of an end-of-the-world scenario. This is the profile of a fool, not the profile of an adventurer, the seeker of wisdom and greatness. Vengeance, getting even, and hanging on to old wounds are also the follies of a fool.

These goals cannot be accomplished overnight, but this is the starting point. The fool above all else hangs onto pain and suffering and perpetuates it at home, at work, everywhere. This never-ending saga of making up and breaking up with the ones we love is foolish nonsense. How silly can we be?

It goes without saying that the fool has no idea what is important and what is not. That is why great teachers such as Lakshmanjoo come into the world to point the way for those who are interested. God comes into the world to give Himself a hand in self-discovery.

Chapter Nine

The Creator/Destroyer

THIS CHAPTER IS ABOUT A NEW BEGINNING, MADE POSSIBLE BY A sharper, clearer image of ourselves. We will delve deeper into the concept of the creator/destroyer, then discuss our sexuality, which is part of our creator impulse. If the information seems to emphasize our negative aspect, that's because the dark half, like the dark side of the moon, has been a stranger to us. Our introduction to that half of our self is long overdue. We have been much more familiar with and accepting of our loving kindness than our potential to express cruelty and violence. If you conceptualize yourself as a saint filled with compassion and love for humanity, that's great. Continue to do so. But from now on, do not overlook your other half.

In the past, whenever I pictured myself, I envisioned my better half and was unaware that my dark side even existed. You know the saying about a wolf in sheep's clothing?

Try to remember the last time you were so angry you were literally out of control. Nothing else existed but absolute rage, right? Say hello to the unabashed nature of your destructive personality. For me, when that personality overtakes me, it causes the veins to pop out on the side of my head, my body to shake, and my voice to quaver. This energy explodes outward and levels everything in its path; my abuse of others is terrible when I am out of control. This destructive personality is always nearby, lurking just behind my conscious awareness. Even when I am feeling calm and all is well, the destroyer is watching, scrutinizing every situation.

The destroyer is so monstrous in size and strength, just thinking about it is appalling. It is the murderer on the streets, the hate monger in the ghetto, the bigots, the racists. It is the roving teenage gangs committing random violence. It is the muscle behind sexual harassment, sarcasm, condescension, back-stabbing, and degradation of others. It is the force behind self-criticism. It is pure destruction! In my opinion, it could slaughter the whole of humanity and never bat an eyelash.

Most people would deny that they are capable of such behavior. "I am not that kind of person," you might say as you read this. But you are. We all have our own special way of expressing this self, and some express it more overtly than others.

The destroyer offers its input to all our choices. If you are among the vast majority who do not live in self-awareness, then the personality in gear at that moment (creator or destroyer) calls the shots, not you. Most people have little if any self-awareness and therefore no control over what is about to happen. Under these circumstances we have no choice in our action or behavior. As each incident of our life happens, we react like puppets on a string, controlled by personalities we do not even know exist. There is no choice here, there is no control; we are merely robots, acting and reacting like complete fools.

The destroyer controls our outward persona much more often than we realize. Every second of every day, this creature takes us hostage and, right under our nose, exerts its will on the events of our lives. All the while, we never have the faintest idea of what is happening. Because our good and bad behaviors are braided like the strands of a rope, the elements of our makeup are difficult to sort out. The fool can never see what is really going on.

Obtaining an unbiased view of human nature is practically impossible. As children we are taught what we "should" be like, so knowing our true self becomes a hopeless pursuit by the age of six or seven. Younger children are the best studies if you want a glimpse at our authentic, uncivilized self. (Age and gender mean nothing; these dual personalities cut across all age groups and both sexes. It is difficult, however, to find an adult who hasn't been taught to suppress unacceptable social behavior.) It is instructive to watch two little kids at play—boy and girl, two boys, two girls. One second they are in love, literally best friends, pretending to get married, cooing, sharing, cooperating. Seconds later they are crying and screaming, punching and scratching, literally in a fit of temper and hate. Except for getting tired and hungry, this is a child's life: back and forth, back and forth, making up and breaking up all day long.

Most parents will not tolerate their children's tantrums and demand an immediate halt to them. "Stop that this instant!" we say. "Big girls don't act like that." "Play nice. Be a good little boy." Nobody wants to be around when the destroyer is on the loose.

Of course we parents have not known until now what we were dealing with when the destroyer surfaced in our children. Naive, we tried to shoo it away. Not understanding that the monster cannot be eliminated, we expect our children to accomplish the impossible. The destroyer stays; the only thing that changes over the years is the program of attack and destroy. No matter what, hatred and destructiveness prevail, to manifest themselves in a more acceptable disguise. Regardless, the destroyer destroys all.

We punish little boys and girls for being the tiny monsters they are; then, in the next breath, as if there were some great and noble purpose for our tearing their heart out, we predict that someday—after they grow up—they will thank us for being so mean. Keep in mind that when we look down at our children, it is both through the destroyer's eyes, filled with hatred, wanting to reprimand and spank, and the creator's, brimming with compassion, understanding, and love. All this happens simultaneously.

Life becomes a chaotic mess at home, at work, and every place because we are all creator/destroyers; one creator/destroyer interacting with another; like monsters out of control and in pain—very dangerous. Without understanding this, how could there be a solution for peace and harmony? Unless we understand, we will never be in a position to have a choice. Unless there is a choice, we can never conquer our own nature. Unless we conquer our own nature, we are stuck in this hell.

Our children are not the only victims of mixed messages. We show no mercy to our own self, either. Does this sound familiar? You wake up in the morning and plan a strategy for perfect health and happiness, but by nightfall you've gone off your diet, been "too busy" to exercise, and are looking for a way to abuse yourself with drugs or alcohol or worse. This type of behavior does not happen because something is wrong with you. Quite the contrary; we all worry about good health, good nutrition, and physical fitness…in between our cigarettes, alcohol, drugs, and overeating or purposeful starvation. One personality is committed to perfect health; the other is fixated on self-annihilation.

We unwittingly do violence to our children and ourselves. What about our spouses? Husbands and wives usually behave graciously at cocktail parties or in public; they act as though they are in love, and they are. But in private, behind closed doors, love is not always guiding their interactions. One way or another, our destroyer makes uninterrupted domestic harmony an impossible dream. The destroyer shatters marital harmony the same way "hate groups" shatter peace on earth.

When love, tenderness, and sensitivity are displayed toward the opposite sex, the moment is fleeting. Nobody has the faintest idea of their composition; who has the faintest idea that they are creator/destroyers and through this personage we act upon the world? We are creator/destroyers, this is our fundamental makeup. No wonder our lives are a living hell. No wonder marriages are a shamble, kids grow up with broken hearts, and the streets of the world are filled with blood.

Religion, popular psychological theories, self-help books, and marriage counseling offer little assistance in curbing these two personalities. There is absolutely no strength in this; knowledge of thy own self is the only way. "Know thyself" is the only foundation one can build on to become powerful and harmonious.

Most people never consider how sexual we are, nor how we were created. To most, Mom and Dad, genetics and fertilization, were it. But that is much too small a picture. The power that blasted the universe out of nothing is the same force that we call our sexuality. We are sexual creatures, inside and out. A huge part of the creator half of our nature manifests itself in our sexuality. The heat of seduction is like a magnet, drawing humans together. We evaluate from a sexual point of view everyone we meet. Our bodies are designed as pleasure-seeking, reproductive instruments, and our minds and hearts are filled with sexual force and direction. When this fully blossoms in teenagers, they are so intoxicated with its force that it turns them into almost total idiots. The sexual tremors we experience are the tip of the iceberg; the immense, submerged base is the collective sexual-creative potency of the universe.

Our sexuality exudes from us in many different forms, with a strength and magnitude we have yet to comprehend. Its glow gives off love, warmth, and charm. Our desire to be attractive to the opposite sex consumes more of our daily concentration than we realize—a new hairstyle, the right clothes, a sensuous perfume or masculine aftershave, an expensive car, a powerful job or impressive professional title—all are intended to make our sexuality noticeable. Otherwise, why would we care about these things? Our self-esteem, our idea of who and what we are, even at the most mundane level, has to do with sexuality. We are sexual creatures to the core of our being.

We have a love-hate relationship with our sexuality, which is twisted in superstition and religion and, subsequently, shame and guilt. Instead of perceiving sexuality as a universal force that powers our life and breath, we despise ourselves for being what we are. Instead of reverence and respect for the magnificence that can transform nothingness into life, we feel ashamed of ourselves. We are Creators and this sexual potency is proof of who we are. Rather than understanding and embracing this creative force that energizes our being, we shun and repress it. It's sad that we attach such stigma to our sexuality. Whether or not we accept it openly, our entire life revolves around it.

On the other hand, our sexual nature gets us into more trouble than we would care to admit. When this force electrifies our being, we become like puppets on a string, losing all control—just as we do when anger and rage take us over. Instead of being aware and in control, we are reduced to the same level as an animal. When the sexual and violent natures join forces, especially in men, it can result in unwanted advances, petty innuendoes, sexual harassment, and rape. Being anything less than a perfect gentleman is totally unacceptable in this philosophy. Keeping the lid on our sexual impulses is just as important as keeping the lid on our anger and violence. The challenge for Shaivite philosophers is to be creator/destroyers and bring their sex and violence under total control, where there is no leakage of these impulses, to conquer the forces of nature within oneself by sheer will.

We humans certainly deny our fascination with violence. Watch or listen to a news program on any given morning and you will hear discussions on topics such as the execution of a murderer the previous evening, a new theory on the entry and exit bullet holes through President John F. Kennedy's head, or an update on police brutality. This is what we wake up to every morning, and it goes on all day long. The media—television, radio, newspapers, news magazines—serves us violence because it captures our interest and satisfies our destroyer's appetite. More than anything else, television feeds us sex and violence twenty-four hours a day on every large network and during every commercial break. If you have not watched music videos on one of the music video cable stations, you might want to watch for a few minutes. Music seems a lesser priority in the programming than sex and violence.

For the most part, humanity can refrain from overt physical violence. Today's events in Central Europe ("ethnic cleansing"), yesterday's World War II, and the more distant Crusades are examples of what happens when "decent, God-fearing" people lose control and commit genocide. As the rage never ceases, every generation in every corner of the world slaughters and butchers each other one way or another, on the battlefield or in the streets. Religious oppression, ethnic infringement, racial misunderstanding—the excuses never end.

CREATOR, PROTECTOR, DESTROYER

Our destructive psychological nature does not always demand such extreme behavior as wielding an ax or knife or shooting a bullet to inflict its wounds. In most households and businesses, brutality rolls off the tip of our tongue in the things we say. We are masters of disparagement. We denigrate ourselves; we are disrespectful; we humiliate our friends; we degrade people a thousand times a day. Naturally we always have some good reason or excuse for our verbal attacks. Nonetheless, the cut is almost as deep as if we had used a blade of steel.

From nine to five, physicians, teachers, priests, senators, judges, all sorts of hardworking people, male and female, contribute to society. By night, many of these same folks turn into something else: abusers of drugs, children, and spouses, whore hounds or collectors of pornography. They put in jeopardy their personal health or life, the integrity and well-being of their family, profession, and reputation. Half their behavior is commendable, productive, and uplifting; the other half teeters on the edge of total destruction and self-annihilation. Fortunately for them, most are not caught red-handed and exposed on the front page of the newspaper for the entire world to read about and condemn. For the majority of us, our dark side is not so demonstrative. Sometimes we are entirely unaware of lapsing into the role of the destroyer. But rest assured, it is there whether you see it or not.

From outward appearances, these fine, upstanding individuals seem in control, the foundation of the very society they serve. As family members, contributors to society, we all fit into this picture. But underneath this superficial facade rests our real nature, the creator/destroyer. This is who we are regardless of outward appearances and this is what determines the overall theme of our life.

I have already mentioned the workplace: sexual harassment, back-stabbing, ruthless manipulation, betrayal...wherever there are people, basically every conceivable underhanded maneuver is taking place. As creator/destroyers with our sex and violence out of control, we shatter the workplace, the happiness and harmony in our homes, and the planet on which we live. The things we do to each other are beyond description. Why? There is no reason except that this personality exists. This thing is insatiable; civilization and sophistication mean nothing. Trying to figure out how to achieve a lasting peace by looking back through history for clues to our perpetual misunderstanding of each other is futile. Peace on any front can only come from understanding the creator/destroyer.

The creator/destroyer is what we are and who we are. How we have been taught to perceive ourselves means almost nothing. Superficial appearances mean nothing. We are this creature, clear and simple. We are complete strangers to ourselves.

What a narrow, limited view we have of reality! Even Sigmund Freud, recognized as the father of modern psychology, was not unlike the rest of us. At age fifty-nine, Freud wrote this letter to J. J. Putnam, a convert to psychoanalysis. Putnam had asked Freud to write about the relationship of morality to psychoanalysis. Freud responded:

> *I think I ought to tell you that I have always been dissatisfied with my intellectual endowment and that I know precisely in what respect, but that I consider myself a very moral human being who can subscribe to Th. Vischer's excellent maxim: "What is moral is self-evident." I believe that when it comes to a sense of justice and consideration of others, to the dislike of making others suffer or taking advantage of them, I can measure myself with the best people I have known. I have never done anything mean or malicious, nor have I felt any temptation to do so.**

* From "Letter to James J. Putnam" (#169) from *Letters of Sigmund Freud,* edited by Ernst L. Freud, Basic Books, 1960.

Freud obviously saw the horrible things people do to one another but could not fathom this sort of behavior coming from himself. Freud was considered a genius, so how could this be? Was he lying? Of course not. He, like all of us, did not monitor his moods and thoughts vigilantly, nor had he disentangled his good from his bad in order to gain a clear picture of both.

As far as I can tell, we are all exactly like Freud. We can see violence everywhere, but we cannot fathom it coming from our own self. Incredibly, this blindness seems to be shared by all; we are unable to observe our own meanness, cruelty, vengeance, aloofness, perpetuation of emotional upset, instability, and despair. This is the fool's plight, absolute and utter self-ignorance.

In order to see the truth, we have to disarm ourselves, put our defensiveness aside, relax, then take a look. This is not a witch hunt or an exercise in self-condemnation; it is a search for truth and power.

Certainly life will be easier now that we actually know what is going on. We will not have to be so serious. We can enjoy each day more than before. Most of us are incredibly serious, and for good reason: a heart filled with disappointment and hurt—failed relationships, rocky marriages, heartbroken children—keeps us in a somber mood. Even though we refuse to admit it, we have a side that wants to destroy everything we set our hands on—and it does.

The creator/sexual aspect of our nature is equally vast and awesome. It is the other half of our essence. From its glow that fills our being, we have affinity toward others. It is this personality that adores and sees the glamour and beauty as it gazes into the eyes of others or its own self. This personality exudes warmth and charm. When its power and energy are under control, it fills the individual with a feeling of well-being and strength. From a perspective that few appreciate, it can turn wrath into compassion and understanding. From this position of total control comes altruism, true caring, understanding, and love. When wielders of this power lose control over it, they become animals and abandon behavior that is uplifting and warm.

Everything we think, say, and do teeters on the edge of good and bad. Each of us acts out his or her own part in how we treat our family, make decisions on the floor of Congress, and negotiate peace or declare war on our fellow human beings. We each contribute to a never-ending charade that hangs on the whim of personalities inside us that we do not even know exist. So pay attention to yourself: Notice how the creator/ destroyer impulse influences your thoughts, emotions, and physical sensations. See how it gives shape to your words, ideas, and actions. You will begin to predict what is about to happen; then, with practice, you will be able to alter its final outcome.

What I am talking about demands clear thinking to comprehend, let alone do something about. Most human minds are so indoctrinated in their current beliefs and complicated theories about what it means to be human that nothing will change them. They will never see how simple this truth really is.

Perhaps you will comprehend this logic, readjust obsolete, useless perspectives, and break through a barrier of ignorance as I have by the grace of Lakshmanjoo. Slowly but surely, it is possible to gain increasing control over the forces of nature. I am doing it.

But first let me tell you about the one other aspect of nature that influences you in both a positive and negative way: It is fear, our protector. It is that which maintains us and inspires the status quo.

Chapter Ten

The Protector

IN THE GREAT STORIES OF KASHMIR SHAIVISM, IT IS SAID THAT EVEN Lord Siva, Supreme God of the Universe, the Creator/Protector/ Destroyer of all that exists, hesitated in a state of apprehension and fear— fear that creating the universe out of His own self would lessen His state of perfection and bliss. Just at the point where the Almighty had the incli- nation to create, He stopped. Then, when the inspiration struck again, He moved forward and created 118 universes and suffered no lessening of His supreme state of perfection and bliss.

This story clearly illustrates that fear and apprehension, along with creation and destruction, are a part of the divine commentary. For every- thing that exists, there is a beginning, middle, and end. In life, fear is what protects and maintains the middle.

CREATOR, PROTECTOR, DESTROYER

Lakshmanjoo once said, "Everything scares me!" But there is a difference between understanding oneself and being in control, and not understanding oneself and being out of control. Even though one experiences fear, being the master of one's own self is the key. Those who do not comprehend the forces of the universe will always remain limited and bound. True, their fear will protect them, as it does for an animal, but it will promote stagnation and maintenance of the status quo. It will keep them small, weak, and timid. This journey toward self-realization takes great courage.

If you look at an X-ray of a Homo sapiens' head, what you will see is the result of two billion years of struggle both as predator and prey: massive armor plating for protection plus an efficient set of teeth and jaws for ripping and chewing. Without our skin and hair, we all look almost identical: skeletons held together and designed for mobility with ligament, tendon, and muscle; energized with blood coursing through a conduit of arteries and veins; fueled with organ systems that take sustenance from plant or animal and convert it into its own energy—robots of sorts.

Skinned, stripped of our veneer of culture and intelligence, we appear as primitive as any other animal that roams the face of the earth in an attempt to sustain its life. To survive, we humans, like every other life form, need a never-ending food supply to stoke the furnace that powers and energizes our being.

It is this creature that is under the control of the creator/protector/destroyer. It is consciousness that gives life, force, and direction to this muscle, bone, and blood. Flesh in itself is nothing; it is dead. Consciousness is what brings it to life. This is who we are, conscious beings trapped within flesh and blood. But rather than remain ignorant of our true composition, it is time to try and comprehend, to take control, to stand on top of these forces instead of being the fool in a fool's drama.

The Protector

This protective force in limited beings manifests itself as fear. It is nothing to be ashamed of; it is something to understand. This is what keeps us alive. At the mundane level of everyday survival, fear is our protector.

Fear is as necessary as our breath. Without it, there would be no life. Were it not for fear, we would walk heedlessly into dangerous situations. Our existence would be over before we even got started.

We need to change our attitudes about the powerful force of fear by increasing our understanding of it. Like our destroyer and creator impulse, the fear response is in our nature; it is who and what we are. Rarely do we realize how scared we are. Fear directs our actions and behavior, but the underlying reasons for our behavior usually remain hidden. Not to understand how fear affects our life is a sentence to mediocrity or worse.

A component of fear is present in absolutely everything we encounter, good and bad. We fear losing the things we treasure. We worry about money, our jobs, our spouses, our health. We worry whether we are getting enough sleep; we can worry ourselves sick over almost anything twenty-four hours a day...or we can worry ourselves sick over nothing. Fear rides like some sort of beast on our neck, shoulders, back, and in our gut, with tight muscles and tension headaches, acrid perspiration, and increased pulse. Just as a gazelle is on the lookout to spring into flight at the first sign or scent of a predator, humans are at the ready; we feel that something or someone is always at our heels.

I remember late-summer nights, when my father would send me to the far corners of the orchards to turn off the irrigation sprinklers. An obedient but terrified ten-year-old, I tried to keep our house's lights in view while I ran as fast as I could across the fields. In my imagination, every shadow concealed a psychopathic murderer and every tree hid a dreadful monster waiting to pounce on me. At each water control, I quickly turned off the valve, then, panting from exertion and fear, I dashed to the next destination. When all four valves were closed, I high-tailed it back to the house. My heart pounded in fright. Inside the security of our back yard, I slowed to a walk and tried to breathe normally and appear nonchalant so no one would suspect I had been panic-stricken. Showing anyone how I really felt would have been too embarrassing.

Fear is why children can be so easily molded. Youngsters worry about alienating parents and being punished. To satisfy their demands, children learn to behave in a socially acceptable manner.

Without fear, there would be no chance of taming or controlling these wild and powerful personalities, the creator and destroyer. This whole existence delicately balances on this triad of inner personalities.

After we grow up, a similar system influences us. We adults obey the laws of society as best we can and pay our taxes in April not because we want to but because we are afraid not to. Imprisonment, fines, and other retributions are strong persuaders. A law-abiding, God-fearing citizen is just that: somebody who is driven by fright.

Like the creative and destructive energies, fear is both good and bad. If it is truly protecting us, it is good. If it is keeping us from advancing in our lives, then it is bad. We fear for our children and thus protect them; we fear for our lives and thus protect ourselves; we fear for many things and this is what keeps us out of harm's way as much as possible. On the other hand, fear is what promotes total stagnation. No matter how low someone may exist, no matter how terrible a life of pain and suffering he or she may lead, there is something contained within this life of hell that the individual is fearful of giving up. Whether it be drugs, alcohol, smoking, or whatever, there is some small amount of joy, some trace of pleasure, some small comfort that the individual is terrified to leave behind.

It is fear that keeps us from moving on to bigger and better things. This will not do for those who are interested in pursuing this grand adventure. This adventure is not for the timid or weak of heart. Therefore we need courage, tremendous courage. Only with courage can we break out of the limited state of being. We have to be willing to give up some of the small pleasures of life in order to obtain something much bigger.

When all three personalities—creator, protector, and destroyer—are together inside one skin, the result is a wild and fantastic creature, unpredictable and dangerous. These three forces spin a web of drama that entangles our life in a mess that is beyond description—a confusion of the mind, pain and suffering. How very strange it is to be such a mixture of personalities. We love the ones we destroy, we protect the ones we love. It does not make sense to the fool. Needless to say, this is why we are all so neurotic. Interacting with one another is quite traumatic. Trying to understand is the key, then doing something about it. That is what this whole adventure is about: It is a challenge to see what you can do. There is work to be done for those who are interested.

The bottom line in any endeavor is courage. There can be no substitute for this; to change, to give up old habits, to create a better, brighter, more powerful existence takes great courage and the refreshed commitment to it each and every day.

Chapter Eleven

God: Recognizing Lord Siva

B Y A TRICK OF HIS OWN MAKING IN AN INCREDIBLE GAME, LORD SIVA purposely contracts Himself into a state of limitation. Shaiva philosophy states that we have to undo the first trick—imposing limitations and forgetfulness—by performing a second trick—realizing what we have done and reconnecting to who we really are. Rediscovering our true identity presents an enormous but exciting challenge to the intellect, imagination, and will: We must rise from this individual state of being to the universal state of being. The practical benefits that come from taking this journey enrich our daily living enormously.

Once we humans begin trying to understand that we are God, the game begins. Understanding this is the point of entry into the divine game. Ultimately, we will become exactly what we believe ourselves to be. We start with a metaphysical understanding and end with a mystical experience.

CREATOR, PROTECTOR, DESTROYER

In the final analysis, our individual state of being is like a magician's sleight of hand—a trick in which nothing has happened at all—simply play within the Consciousness of God. It only appears that something has occurred or changed—God is still God and never anything but God. It has always been so; it is so now, and it always will be so. Remember, Consciousness is undividable, unchangeable, and immutable. Even as individual beings, we are made from this divine Consciousness, which is our composition and makes us who we are. Even though we cannot experience our connectedness to the surrounding world, it is an expansion of our own being. Until we experience this Truth, our spiritual work is not done.

Belief in the divine Consciousness is to be held quietly within the heart and mind and not boasted about to others. The practice of this philosophy is basically secretive. Shaivites are doers, not talkers. Actions speak for themselves. Except for my writing, I have nothing to say to anybody but my family. This practice is to be lived.

I try to keep my belief in the forefront of my awareness all day long and believe in it. I try to establish firmly in my own mind that this whole existence is an expansion of my own self. This requires a great leap of faith. Fortunately, faith grows over time. I also try to follow a strict moral code of behavior.

As the realization of our own divinity grows and becomes resolute, worry and grief melt away. If God does not experience pain and suffering, why should we? To make this work, I try to remember that principle as I move through the day. For example, if something bad has just happened, I have two choices: I can either enjoy it as part of Lord Siva's divine play or react to it in a fit of horror and disbelief. Those who understand that Lord Siva rests behind all of the events that occur in our life can develop a new way to react based on this understanding; his or her life changes completely. This is detachment, this is how to give up this world and still be a part of it. Even this detachment is a trick; one trick deserves another. Detachment is a state of mind, a special way of looking at the world and a special way of reacting to it.

As you progress in your spiritual journey, you become happy and content and develop a genuine peace of mind. This transformation is quite amazing, actually; joy comes from moving away from the world, not embracing it. Rather than connect with every little detail that becomes a part of life, relax and see the awe-inspiring superdrama that unfolds right before our eyes—Lord Siva's play. Every bit of it is His doing. We do the best we can and the rest is up to Him. Why not worship this divine saga? See God as the one responsible for every detail of it. Worship the good as well as the bad. In this way there can be joy in our hearts no matter what is going on. Bad news, good news—who cares?

The way I believe and think, every word that is spoken to me and every event that befalls me—including table conversation with my wife and daughter and chitchat with my patients—is a direct interaction with Lord Siva. This is a wonderful way to view the world; it makes life exciting, more intriguing, and more powerful.

Why should we feel so attached to worldly possessions? After all, if everything that exists is God, and we are God, then the entire universe is our own self. Why covet what we already have? This is extremely important for advanced students. Fixation on the material world keeps us earthbound and in a state of limitation, just as our passion does. Who can deny our fanatical preoccupation with the need for this or that? These thoughts fill our head all day long. The wise do not care either way; they can take it or leave it. They are the same.

Why be jealous? The Shaivite philosopher sees other individuals as an expansion of his or her own self, so what is there to be jealous of? If we

97

are God, what is there to be jealous of? Who could we be jealous of? The correct answer is nothing and no one. This is how I think when feelings of jealousy take me over. Not feeling jealous takes practice, but you will be surprised how fast you can change when you have kept at it.

Shaivite philosophy has no room for anger, either, for even our so-called enemies are a part of us and are themselves divine. All behaviors—both good and bad—are our own acts, because everything is an expansion of our own self. A Shaivite practitioner would listen to the stories on the evening news and think, "I did that. Those are my deeds, my acts." Adopting this outlook has been very helpful to me as I work to change my limited perception and begin to realize fully the concept of the divine self. It also helps develop a much more compassionate outlook toward this world and the creatures and people who fill it.

As this new vantage point develops, we can become truly compassionate, forgiving, and appreciative of the human predicament. Only by picturing ourselves as divine and interconnected can we become truly great—so much more than the small, limited, powerless, vulnerable beings we mistakenly think ourselves to be. We have to start thinking big now, really big.

Our goal is to become Lord Siva fully realized.

The first step is to intellectualize this new identity as the creator/protector/destroyer and take control of our being, to bring our sexual nature under control and become courageous and nonviolent. Refinement is the key. This requires practice and constant remembrance of the self as divine.

Followers of Kashmir Shaivism make a concerted effort to remain fully cognizant of their own divinity and the divinity of everyone and everything else. That means that dogs, cats, birds, worms, chairs, cars—everything—is Lord Siva. Humans, however, with their self-awareness, are the only entities who can know the nature of their true self. A dog, for example, cannot know that it is Lord Siva.

This knowledge accomplishes two things. First, it adjusts how we perceive ourselves: God is everything; nothing exists that is not God, and that includes each and every one of us. Second, the recognition of the divinity of all things influences all our relationships. We begin to feel a great connection to other people, to animals, and to the environment. I am Lord Siva; you are Lord Siva; my pet is Lord Siva. God enjoys and personally plays all the roles for all things, animate and inanimate. With this great knowledge and new perspective, true change can occur.

How could this wisdom not affect our relationships with someone as close to us as our mate and children, or as distant as a stranger in another car on the freeway? Nothing is more powerful. This is the ultimate lesson.

Most people wait a lifetime for a compassionate God to relieve them of their pain and suffering when in fact we are God; we are the ones who should be compassionate and understanding of the universal predicament. This is the trick. We humans have everything backward; this is part of the trick.

If I am God, and if this universe and all of its individual parts are an expansion of my own self, then it is my responsibility as God to treat my creations with tenderness, compassion, and love. Even my enemies should be viewed as part of my own self. This is the correct way of thinking. Ethics and morality take on a whole new dimension in this context.

Chapter Twelve

Becoming Nonviolent

IF YOU ARE WILLING TO GIVE SHAIVA PHILOSOPHY A TRY, THEN GET SET for a grand adventure. You will work toward developing an ever-powerful will, choosing your actions, and being in charge of your life.

As individuals, even though ignorant of what and who we are, we are nonetheless the three personalities of the creator, protector, and destroyer. For the most part, these personalities rest outside our awareness and the reasons behind our behavior remain hidden. Most of the time we simply do not know why we do what we do. We act thoughtlessly, then are forced to sift through the wreckage to salvage whatever we can of our health, marriage, career, and so on.

These personalities are responsible for the upheaval and chaos in our lives. We are robots for a controller we do not even know exists. Mischievous havoc is played out in marriage, raising children, kids playing, territorial aggression, politics, and in every conceivable occurrence in our lives. It is not our drama, it is their drama.

We are all fools in a fool's drama. We have no idea why we wind up in our predicaments, one after the other, day in and day out. From leaders of nations and religions to the lowest of the low, there are few exceptions. Even though we are conscious and have the ability to think, we are cut off from the real personalities that direct our lives.

We go to counselors, healers, psychiatrists, and others, looking for answers and relief from our great afflictions. The secret to this dilemma is simply understanding. With this great knowledge, we can learn to choose our behavior. Now, with a choice, we can change everything. Knowing who and what we are means everything. We have to know before we can work with it.

Until now we believed that our behaviors were directed by a clear, unbiased, intelligent mind. Not so! To our great detriment, the real decision making in our life is accomplished outside our awareness, where we have no control over it. Thoughts, feelings, emotions, moods, everything we are consciously aware of originates within those three personalities. As the wants and whims of the three personalities surface in our awareness, what is about to happen—what you are about to say and how you are about to behave—has already been decided and is well on its way to completion before we have the faintest inkling. Until we accept this, we are completely at the mercy of a mind we do not even know exists.

Without making a concerted effort to monitor the wants and whims flowing freely from the creator/protector/destroyer, we have no chance of establishing a lasting peace with others. If something happens before we can get a handle on it, we will never be in a position to make a choice. Most of what comes to be (as far as our behavior is concerned) seems more like knee-jerk reactions. It just happens; then we blow up, panic, get angry, make derogatory put-downs, inflammatory accusations, and inappropriate advances. It just seems to happen all by itself, so where is the choice? If we are never in a position to make a choice, we will continue to move from one personal interaction to the next, with good action and bad action. Marriages become a living hell, children are shattered, the world is annihilated.

There is no way we can dominate our titanic psychological impulses, but we can change the final shape they take as their commands move outward through our body, mind, and soul. With practice and discipline, we can choose our behavior. Bringing our sexual and violent natures under control is our goal—to conquer what we are.

My intent is to express only goodness and good action. I practice keeping the lid on my sexual and violent behaviors. I keep close track of what I am doing as I interact with others at home, in the workplace—everywhere. Ultimately, anything short of being a perfect gentleman or gentlewoman is not good enough. Some might think by today's standards that this type of behavior is unfashionable or a sign of weakness. On the contrary! I am talking about becoming the Conqueror—the epitome of strength—becoming more powerful than anything else that exists.

Obviously, achieving these ends has practical benefits for us, our family and friends, and the whole world. Unfortunately, we have few role models for this type of behavior. Wanting to live by a personal set of ethics and doing so are two different things. I have met only one person who was wholly good, and that was Lakshmanjoo. He taught me that in order to master our behavior, we must exert self-control—willpower.

"Control over what?" you might ask. Finding the answer to that question brings us to facing the truth about our own selves. We must learn to identify our psychological impulses.

Focus on yourself and see clearly what you are. As you undertake this step, you will begin to recognize which of the three personalities is expressing itself through you at any given moment.

To take control and become nonviolent, you need awareness of what is going on inside yourself, forgiveness, and to live in the moment.

First, monitor what you are about to do and listen to what you are about to say. See and hear what is coming, and in so doing, you will change your life forever. To expand your awareness, turn your attention upon your inner self. Try to focus on what is going on inside your own being. Become aware. You must be focused on yourself at all times, no matter what else you are doing. While you interact with others, talk, or drive your car, have your mind's eye focused on your own state of being. This is awareness. Outward focus is meaningless and powerless; inward focus (starting with moods, thoughts, emotions, and actions) is where the pot of gold lies.

As we become increasingly aware of our thoughts and impulses and how they mold our behavior into good action or bad action, we must be prepared to leap over a hurdle. New students of Kashmir Shaivism often experience difficulty identifying their destroyer tendencies. They never picture themselves as violent, hateful creatures, and for good reason: They overlook subtle violence. Any aggression short of a knife fight may be perceived as nasty, distasteful, or crude, but not violent. I have already said that most brutality in our society is expressed in what we say. The full force of the creator/protector/destroyer can be delivered through our speech, from the tone of our voice to subtle double meanings, from joking innuendoes to overt derogatory verbal assault. Everyone is involved in this drama. What a twisted, tangled mess, fools in a fool's drama. Although we do not chop up our husbands or wives or children with an ax, we do it with the words that roll off our tongues.

When we are the target of someone else's bad action—be it hidden or expressed—we often mistakenly believe that the person is being purposely malicious. This person is not in any more control than you are. (Of course, if we are involved in bad action, we believe we are justified.) The victim and the victimizer blame each other.

It is up to us as individuals to untangle ourselves from chaos. We must stop blaming others for the unhappiness we feel; we must forgive—and this is the second step toward gaining peace of mind. Except on rare occasions, people do not plan bad action toward one another. We cannot blame a dog or a cat for being the way it is, and we cannot hold humans responsible for doing something over which they have absolutely no control. This is a no-fault philosophy. No one is to blame for our predicament—except God.

The second step toward becoming nonviolent is knowing that it is not necessary to take offense when others behave badly. Remind yourself that the actions of others are beyond their control. Excuse them for it. Most people have absolutely no idea what or who they are or how they are affecting those around them. Therefore, those who cannot forgive or who choose to hold vengeance in their heart will never understand this teaching, nor will they ever make any progress in it. You have to start someplace, and this is that place: forgiveness.

There is no other way but to be compassionate and forgiving of others' ignorance and actions. Forgiveness is a challenge to see how powerful one can become. Anybody can carry a grudge or vengeance in their heart. Forgiveness is something we do for ourselves. Otherwise our lives are diminished to never-ending dramas of being hurt and getting even. Forgiveness is a difficult lesson to learn. With practice we can develop our patterns in the same way that a weight lifter develops muscles—by going into training on a committed, long-term basis. This may sound simple, but it is not. To control the powers within us, we have to train.

Nothing is sweeter than the self-satisfaction of exerting our will over the whims of the personalities that savor the good as well as the bad. Every time we enjoy a victory by swallowing a cruel remark before it escapes our lips, our trophy is knowing that we have moved on a true and straight path for one of the first times in our life. Every time we halt the release of another inappropriate sexual overture to a friend or coworker, or turn down promiscuity or unfaithful behavior, we are on our way to refinement and power. In my own struggle, I have come a long way. Even though I still have my ups and downs, my power is increasing day by day.

The third step toward making peace with who we are and becoming nonviolent is to concentrate our attention on the here and now. This is where true power originates and the only time we get to know ourselves directly. Our awareness must be directed to the fleeting split-second of the moment. I have become a dispassionate observer of who I am as each moment passes. It takes constant alertness to keep track of oneself and every impulse, movement, and feeling that rises from the creator/destroyer as it hits the surface and before it takes shape in words and actions. By learning to monitor ourselves with awareness, we can change into a different being.

The sole point in time over which we have any control is the Now. It is in the Now that we plant the seeds for the future. It is only in the instant of the Now that we meet these personalities head-on; otherwise, it is too late. The choice in the matter is gone. We have lost our chance.

By sheer will, the key is to take control, no matter what. There is no way we can do this unless we understand that life is a setup. Just being here in the first place is a setup. In truth, we are little more than pawns in a game: the game of life. Ordinary people, the playthings for this game, are basically idiots, total fools for the real personalities that have no shame or restraint. Winning a Nobel Prize, becoming president, developing some new technology to benefit humanity—without self-knowledge these individuals have nothing; they are still fools.

Those looking for greatness can begin to maintain a true and straight course. With ever-increasing strength of will and awareness, they strive toward good action only. It takes great strength and perseverance to do this. I know from my own experience.

This is why we are here, to see what we can achieve.

Chapter Thirteen

Communication

THE MAIN REASON WE CANNOT GET ALONG WITH ONE ANOTHER IS because of the way we communicate with each other. If, after reading this book, you come away with nothing other than this understanding, your life will change completely, as mine has.

The main reason we do not get along with one another is because we usually communicate at a very primitive level: from the gut. These visceral reactions are actually the reactions of the creator/protector/destroyer. For example, some discussions between a husband and wife stray far from calm, cerebral, intelligent conversation. Why? Because we are more like monsters than refined and wise beings. We are creatures and our message is usually pretty simple; our way of communicating is more often than not a mixture of affection, fear, and rage. Powerful forces shoot back and forth instead of simple conversation. Instead of unemotional, straightforward talk, we are either declaring war, knotted up with fear or terror, or trying to make up. Many times, within two seconds after the first person opens his or her mouth, everything is out of control. It is impossible to be nice, considerate, understanding, and compassionate. This is not the way we are; only a fool would believe this to be so. We are creators/protectors/destroyers and nice is not part of our profiles. I think children must wonder if their parents are from another planet. Isn't "normal" the way families are portrayed on television shows such as *Leave it to Beaver, Father Knows Best,* or *Ozzie and Harriet?*

Of course, this thinking is ridiculous. Out of control and having no idea about who or what we are, parents are more like "things"—and they shatter the harmony of their home and the hearts of their children—simply because it is impossible to carry on a simple conversation with one another. It is no wonder we all live in our own private hells, each of us totally alone, perpetually in a state of recovery from the last beating we received. Harmony is an impossible dream when we live in a constant state of hurt and betrayal. We can rarely express the simplest of wants or share a moment of the day for fear of provoking this monstrous thing.

Most philosophers and psychologists would have us believe that the reason for this barrier between male and female has something to do with gender. "He does not understand me because I am a woman" or "She does not understand me because I am a man." This is not true. This is the furthest thing from the truth! Undoubtedly, there are some differences between the psyches of men and women. Nobody would care to refute this. However, the main reason men and women do not get along is not because of any differences attributable to their gender; on the contrary, the reason they cannot get along is because, in a much bigger picture, they are exactly alike; they are both creators/protectors/destroyers. In this respect they are identical; this defines the true nature of our personalities and explains why we cannot communicate. We are like two titanic personalities crashing into one another.

Whose fault is this? Of course, it is God's fault. Lord Siva dives into this realm of ignorance and becomes the fool in a fool's drama. But He still carries with Him that which He is, the creator/protector/destroyer. But now as the fool with no sense about anything, He is stupid, unrefined, and unknowing of his own self, the fool. Having only this brute force at His disposal in His limited state of being, He operates on the world with the passion contained with these three personalities.

Naturally, the outlet for most of this passion for civilized men and women comes through our speech. We tear each other apart with our words and when we are done communicating with one another, nobody usually has the faintest idea what just happened. Unfortunately, when a husband and wife are through with one another, any witnesses, namely children, are in a state of shock and disbelief; everyone stands knee-deep in the remains of an emotional frenzy.

But this can all change. Just because we are this creature does not mean we have to act like this. That is what is so fantastic; with a little knowledge we can change our behavior completely.

Now that you know what is happening, you can learn to interact with others in new and different ways—that is, if you are willing to take a chance. Tenderness, understanding, compassion, even love can exist. On this worldly plane nothing is more powerful than a true partnership between men and women.

Now that I know who I am and what I am, I have put the lid on these potent forces. Now I talk to my wife in a soft, quiet, caring, intellectual manner so whatever we are trying to accomplish can be solved together as a team. This communication takes control, practice, awareness, and willpower; but it can be done. Instead of licking wounds and getting even, I accomplish something. We are working as a team as parents, a loving couple, and partners in life. We are creators/protectors/destroyers, but we do not have to act out each detail of our lives with the potency of a senseless creature.

The ultimate challenge is purity of body, mind, and speech. Learning how to communicate and talk in a civilized manner in spite of who we are is the challenge. It is a challenge that offers tremendous reward for those who can do it. Husband and wife should both agree to a plan. Lighten up and relax, see the humor in this situation and then, in a light-hearted way, get a kick out of admitting our true nature to one another. It can be fun, a lot of fun. Then go for the control. When things go out of control it should be agreed upon that either person can intercede with a reminder of what is going on—then there should be a laugh and a new beginning. This is how I do it. It works like magic!

The problem is not only between husband and wife, but between father and son, mother and daughter, father and daughter, and mother and son. The whole family should be aware of what is going on. This knowledge is fantastic, for those who would use it.

Chapter Fourteen

Believers

SO-CALLED PRIMITIVE AND ANCIENT CULTURES WERE POLYTHEISTIC; that is, they believed in many gods. They had a deity for the sun and another for the moon, a god for the rain, a god for war, and a goddess of fertility. Over the millennia, people became monotheistic and believed in one God.

Christians, Jews, Muslims, and most all of the other great religions of the world claim to be monotheistic. To them, there is the divine and that which is not divine—everything else, including us impure and flawed human beings. This is not monotheism.

The idea that there are some things that are divine and others that are not is humanity's downfall. It is no wonder there are so many agnostics and atheists. It is no wonder there are so many who say they believe but are not exactly sure in what. Of course, being evil and flawed is tough to swallow. Although religion has been a powerful force in taming human beings, in my opinion, it has a tendency to break their spirit. Rather than leading to self-discovery, religion shatters personal identity. Instead of creating a burning desire to want to understand more about spirituality, it makes the process painful.

The true meaning of monism is simply this: There is God, and that is all. Nothing else exists. Period. In a way, the ancients were closer to the mark because their deities encompassed the good and the bad—love and war, for instance. There is no other theory or philosophy more exciting or powerful. This is the ultimate. Why? Because it is about you—no one other than yourself.

It is difficult at first to grasp how big this concept is, because it is all-encompassing. Nothing exists outside it. Absolutely everything, from the most minuscule to the vast universe, from the highest to the most unmentionable lowest, is just one thing: God. The good, the bad, the creative, the destructive, love, hate, sex, violence, you, and me—everything is divine. The creator/protector/destroyer's presence is everywhere. This is monotheism and the basis of the Kashmir Shaivism philosophy: God is everything. Not only is God everything, God is responsible for everything. "If something is not going right in your life," Lakshmanjoo used to say, "don't blame it on somebody else; blame it on God."

Manifest or unmanifest, good or bad, up or down, life or death, real or unreal, all is play within Lord Siva's divine Consciousness. This Consciousness is the fundamental primordial seed that gives rise to all things. In the final analysis, nothing really happens at all. Consciousness just is. Although we cannot appreciate this by firsthand experience, there is really no such thing as death.

One night, after listening to her bedtime story, my daughter (then only two or three years old) began to weep piteously. My wife and I asked why her heart was so heavy. It had been a perfect day and her intense sadness did not make sense to us. Our daughter said several times that she did not want to tell us what was wrong, but after a little gentle coaxing, she explained that someday Grandma and Grandad, even Mom and Dad would die. This was all related through a great deal of sobbing. I tried to explain to my daughter that even though the body dies, the spirit lives forever and that to our spirit there is no such thing as death. I added that because our hearts are filled with so much fear, it is difficult for us to believe or understand that the body means nothing. Our daughter listened intently, and I knew that in the recesses of her mind she knew that what I said was true. Soon she was fast asleep.

For good reason there are many who believe spirituality is simply wishful thinking by a frightened and fragile creature who has no other choice but to face death.

How terrible is this misunderstanding between humans and their Maker. How lonely and desolate an existence not to have some true appreciation for God and for ourselves.

Obviously, our relationship to God is far more intimate than most could imagine in their wildest dreams. Even our greatest thinkers had absolutely no idea about God or spirituality. How could they? There was nobody to teach them, to inform them, to tell them the secrets of life, to explain to them who and what they are. Except for this veil of ignorance and limitation, we are the Lord. How could they have known this?

Now that we know, at this point in our understanding, life could become really exciting. At this stage of the game it is up to us.

Now that we know, it is time to do something about it, and that is work. According to Lakshmanjoo, the will is everything. If you do not know this, then you are nothing; you are lost. Until you are aware of this at an intellectual level and exert your will, you will have nothing to do with anything. You will remain a puppet on a string. Whether you are a nuclear physicist, the pope, the president, or the lowest of the low, all is irrelevant. Knowing what you are and who you are and then bringing yourself under control, conquering the forces of nature within yourself, is everything. Conquering the atom means nothing compared to conquering your own self. You are the atom, the sun, the moon, the galaxies. All this is contained within your own self. This is what I have learned from Lakshmanjoo's teachings.

Good things happen to us by God's grace. Whether it is in the realm of everyday living or progress in meditation, God helps those who are simple, and simple are those who appreciate this grand adventure. God meets those who refine their behavior and offers them protection and a helping hand. Otherwise God anxiously waits…one lifetime into the next, waiting and waiting and playing. I can tell you firsthand that wanting to change or trying to change does not work. Ultimately, you have to do it before you enjoy divine assistance or acts of grace.

Our false beliefs pertaining to God are extremely shallow. After all, who has had the opportunity for access to one such as Lakshmanjoo? Not many until now, and by His Grace He has opened the door to this greatest of all philosophies to all of the world.

God is an infinitely playful and mischievous being. Life, which seems like serious business to us, is really just a game—divine amusement and excitement. God can do anything He pleases. The Almighty can even be a total fool. "Surely," Lakshmanjoo once told me, "the world is filled with fools! Just look around you."

Once while driving down a Los Angeles freeway with me, Lakshmanjoo pointed to a big, hairy, ugly looking guy riding a Harley Davidson and asked, "Do you think he knows that it is Lord Siva riding that motor-cycle?" To me this statement means that this whole existence, everything and everyone, is simply Lord Siva in disguise.

Even the most foolish among us can undergo a positive transformation by learning who and what we are, then applying our will to control our own destiny. People who live with no awareness come and go as if they were characters in a television soap opera or, worse, stage props in this divine drama: lonely strangers looking for love, even though it is all around them. Desperation, hopelessness, and suffering exist in the midst of plenty.

Chapter Fifteen

Practical Advice as I Live It

BY PAYING CLOSE ATTENTION TO MY REAL PERSONALITIES, I HAVE greater self-knowledge and self-control. My goal is to conquer nature from the inside out and in all areas: at home, in the workplace, everywhere I go, and with everyone I meet.

This chapter builds on that objective by concentrating on practical advice for interactions with family, society, and the world. It offers both general and specific information that has helped me modify my lifestyle, and may help you change yours. Some changes are natural, sensible, and easy; you can integrate them immediately. Other changes challenge your commitment, demand willpower, and may require years of effort before you succeed.

Ten years ago, I realized that everyone could appreciate the spiritual concepts of Shaiva philosophy and find them helpful—these concepts were not just for those on their final leg of self-realization. Actually, learning these concepts is the first step in the grand journey. You must start some-place, and this is where I began. Most people believe that spirituality or Yoga is something to be practiced thirty minutes or so a day, encompassing some sort of meditation or a stretching, strengthening, and limbering rou-tine called asans. The philosophy of Kashmir Shaivism is something you practice all day long. This is Karma Yoga, yoga in action. Awareness at all times is the real practice of Yoga.

Let's begin with the family, because if a person has a safe and loving home, outside difficulties and frustrations seem more endurable and much less important. Outside of personal self-discovery, nothing is more impor-tant than family—nothing. When a whole family adheres to the same phi-losophy, the home becomes a secure haven. No one is too young or too old to participate. My daughter understood the split in her personality by the time she was five. I continue to alert her to the two sides in other people's behavior, and in a loving, nonjudgmental way, I point them out in her own actions. Occasionally I joke with her and her mother about being the sweetest-meanest people I know. They both get a kick out of it and under-stand precisely what I mean. A sense of humor is absolutely necessary.

Any changes you make in your behavior will have a ripple effect on your loved ones—it certainly did in my family. I rearranged my priorities so I would have the energy and desire to put my family and home first. I realized that caring for them is to serve God. Everything I do is to serve God. My wife and I have a clean home. We try to make it cheerful. Refinement, which applies to every aspect of our lives, begins with a neat and tidy home.

I practice patience with my family members and maintain an atti-tude that they can do no wrong. In my eyes, they cannot. I pretend that my loved ones are delicate and easily breakable and try to see that no harm or hurt comes to them, especially from me.

I see my wife as beautiful and godlike. I respect her so much that the thought of speaking down to, belittling, or behaving disrespectfully toward her is inconceivable to me. My child receives the same consideration. I picture myself and them as divine beings—healthy, vital, and strong. We are the creators/protectors/destroyers, powerful and noble beings, self-understood and in control of the powers that be. This is what we really are, so why not practice seeing ourselves in this way?

The challenge begins in the morning when I roll out of bed. If I awaken in a bad mood, I mold my behavior so it will be gentle and uplifting, creating a pleasant atmosphere for those around me. Even when I am feeling angry and short-tempered, I pretend to be otherwise. I practice letting no anger leak from my being. Instead of causing or contributing to my family's sadness or stress, I shower my home with love. I try to be powerful and kind, not powerfully brutal.

I learned a lesson from my daughter just after her second birthday. Late one night, I was exhausted and wanted her to go to sleep. She wanted to stay up later. I told her sharply to get into bed. She said to me, "Don't speak to me in that tone of voice." I haven't since.

When I take the time to imagine what rests behind those big, dark brown eyes of hers, how could I be anything but kind and respectful—even reverent—toward the one who is staring back at me? In my opinion, all parents should try to have this attitude toward their children and each other. If you cannot understand love, then forget love; reverence is the key. What I am talking about is the development of a feeling in your heart that compels you to get down on your knees and bow to the divine being in your spouse or children. Children should be treated as the divine beings they are. The worship of God is all-encompassing for those who understand. So why not truly worship your children?

I have become much more sensitive to how my family members respond to me when we are conversing. When I interact with my wife, sometimes she listens contentedly; other times she backs away from me as if I were some animal from hell. I never understood the differences in her attitude. Now I know that I was in two opposite frames of mind while delivering my end of the conversation. On the surface all was well; there was no anger that I realized. But underneath was a subtle hostility, and this was coming through loud and clear to my wife as pure violence.

The reverse is also true. I used to feel fear as much as anger when my wife openly expressed her rage. I believed that I was on the receiving end of an inflammatory, derogatory, disrespectful put-down. Instead of seeing her as a multitude of personalities, each expressing themselves in the only way they could, I would retaliate in kind. Similarly, we take it as a personal insult when our children are acting up. From personal experience, my best advice is to be compassionate and understanding when your family member's destroyer personality is in control. Because I recognize the destroyer in my wife, I am not mystified by what is happening. Thus, the danger and fear are removed for me.

Before I speak, I know what I am saying, hear how I am saying it, and remember to whom I am saying it. I have learned that by following these suggestions, I can enjoy a more positive relationship with my wife as well as with everyone else.

When under attack by a friend or family member, I try to maintain my state of being so as not to get drawn into a dog-and-cat fight. I use willpower to hold my position, and then I observe what happens. I try to set an example. As Lakshmanjoo was for us, it is now our turn to become the role model; there are so very few.

Possibly the greatest changes that have occurred in my home as a result of this philosophy have to do with raising my child. Most adults would argue that civilizing children—molding a rough and coarse little one into a perfect social being—requires force and harshness. The message from the parent is loud and clear: "I'll turn you into a perfect human being even if it kills you!" In parenting, rather than being a fool in a fool's drama, I try to set the example by my own behavior. Instead of becoming upset by my child's behavior, I bring myself under control. In my opinion, it is better to teach by actions than by words. That is why many parents, preachers—even presidents—have no personal power unless they are already firmly established in the principles they teach. Otherwise, they are just perpetuating the fool's drama.

It is impossible to suppress, bury, or beat the creator/protector/destroyer out of a child. It is crucial that children be taught to appreciate and understand that they have these three sides to their nature. It is incumbent upon parents to teach their little ones who they are, show them how to feel proud of themselves, and instruct them in methods for working with their impulses—just as we work with our own impulses. My wife and I do the best we can to set an example and explain what we are trying to do.

When somebody is being nasty to me and I can respond with genuine respectful consideration, then I feel that I have reached a new level of enlightenment. Although the other person would like to have my head on a platter, I remember with whom I am interacting. If the only thing I am aware of is my ego whining, "He/she is being mean to me," I will probably feel upset and wonder if there is any justice in this world. The challenge then becomes to expand my conceptualization of what is really going on, appreciate the oneness we both share, and forgive. This does not mean that I would not protect myself from physical harm if it came to that.

Good action also means maintaining my own physical integrity. I do my best to break self-destructive habits. I am constantly trying to build my body and breath and become strong and fit. You have to lift yourself up with your own muscle and bone and become their master.

I began this training by obliterating alcohol, cigarettes, and recreational drugs from my life forever. Except for prescription drugs, the only substances that pass between my lips are healthy food and perhaps an occasional pain reliever. If you suffer from chronic health problems or depression, make an appointment with your physician or psychiatrist. There is nothing wrong with taking medication to get yourself healthy again.

Will power develops proportionately to physical conditioning, overall health, and amount of rest. The best program for physical fitness is a rigorous cardiovascular workout. The goal should be to achieve a state that induces perspiration, then maintain it for at least twenty-five to thirty minutes a minimum of three to four times per week. There are many activities that give me a good workout, but brisk walking and swimming are my favorites. Those who have physical limitations should do the best they can. I consider myself in training, both mentally and physically.

One step I took long ago that is beneficial to both spiritual and physical well-being simultaneously is giving up eating meat. Now that I know what rests behind the eyes—not only in humans but in all life—I believe that eating another living, breathing, feeling creature is a violent act. I cannot blame a tiger for eating meat, nor can I blame a human who is ignorant of the divinity of all God's creatures. But now that I know, I am a strict vegetarian. Most people refuse to recognize the violence or the total disrespect inherent in eating meat. "It is already dead by the time it gets to my plate," they rationalize. "I did not kill it." In this case, who shoots the critter is a moot point; whose teeth are chewing it?

When I imagine the violence implicit in the law of the food chain—eat or be eaten—I shudder. Yet it is the most fundamental mandate on earth. Life lives off death. If you want to see this rule in action, watch a few nature documentaries or step out into your back yard. This whole existence is a dinner table. Humans eat at this table like all other life forms. We eat anything we can get our hands on. This is bad, very bad. If there are some things we should truly fear, eating meat is one of these things. Those who eat meat get eaten one way or the other.

After being conditioned since childhood to feel comfortable about eating meat, seeing the truth was not easy at first. I did not grow up in a vegetarian household. I participated in the 4-H club and believed that consuming flesh was a natural thing to do. I was particularly divided in my perspective because one of my 4-H projects was to raise an animal, usually a steer or heifer, which I would love and nurture—and then eat. Only the creator/protector/destroyer could do this.

Becoming a vegetarian is not really so unusual. Think for a moment about how children relate to animals. Children watch cartoon characters that are animals, play with stuffed animals, and are fascinated by real animals. I cannot think of any living being—except for a parent—whom children love more. There is an almost one-pointed fixation on all warm, fuzzy creatures. And yet children eat animals! Like their parents, they wield a knife and fork to slice through an animal's flesh, chew it, and swallow it. Cows, calves, sheep, lambs, chickens, deer, pigs, rabbits—these are the same animals their parents will be reading about in those charming bed-time stories.

Few parents think beyond the magical fairy-tale life the animals enjoy in these nighttime tales. In reality, many of those dancing, laughing, happy creatures in our children's libraries endure a horrible, penned-in subsistence before being brutally butchered in a slaughterhouse.

My daughter has never eaten meat—except for a chicken nugget her four-year-old cousin stuck in her mouth when she was twelve months old. My child chewed one time, then spat it out. When she was two years old, she explained her actions: She had not eaten the nugget "because the animal was still in the meat!"

According to Lakshmanjoo, those who eat meat are plagued by family feuds, unhappiness, misunderstandings, and betrayal. Until they become vegetarians, they will not enjoy peace of mind, family harmony, or personal contentment. I believe that giving up meat must be the top priority for those who want to become powerful. Otherwise, what we eat will eat us, one way or the other. It should be pointed out that a strict vegetarian diet alone will not change one's life. It takes more—much more. On the other hand, those who eat flesh, no matter what they do, will experience pain and suffering, consumed by circumstances that cannot be fixed.

We know that approximately half of all marriages today end in divorce, and the statistic for infidelity is even higher—so high, in fact, that we can assume that many philanderers are content in their marriage and have no thought of divorce. Why, then, are adults tempted to break their marriage vows?

When we are irresistibly attracted to someone other than our mate—be it simple physical arousal or love—we would do well to remember this: Regardless of who the person might seem to be on the surface, that person is an expansion of our own self. Rather than fill ourselves with the desire to act upon that person, we should marvel at our own expansive beauty.

Few people really know what love is, although we all talk about it, think about it, and crave to receive it and give it. Why, then, are our fantasies about love and the reality of what we experience so disparate? Because we are creators/protectors/destroyers. This is the true nature of our personality. Relationships are the drama of two creators/protectors/destroyers getting together. The real attraction between two people, the true desire, is the thrill of seduction and the excitement of complete and utter destruction. Isn't that what relationships are really about—sex and violence? Isn't the passion between two people a cyclone of love/hate/fear? Now that I know what I am and who I am, I know that it does not have to be like that. With restraint and understanding, the creator/protector/destroyer is capable of more, much more. The pleasure and passion of sex and violence are nothing when compared to this new understanding.

This wisdom has practical as well as spiritual applications. It can save a marriage by giving the partners a new perspective. After assimilating this intellectually, spouses soon realize that they do not need to look any further for their life's companion. He or she is gazing at us already when we peer into the eyes of our spouse, when we stare at ourselves in the mirror or look upon our children. The same being exists in all of us. The only thing to do is to bring our creator/protector/destroyer under control and serve our family in a way befitting them. We gain nothing by searching for love somewhere else.

The following lines of Chinese mysticism pertaining to Tao illustrate the true meaning of Love:

Thou knowest not what is love, nor what it is to love. I will tell thee; love is nothing other than the Rhythm of Tao.

I have said it to thee, it is from Tao that thou comest; it is to Tao that thou shalt return. Woman reveals herself to thy eyes and thou thinkest that she is the end toward which the Rhythm leads thee, but even when this woman is thine and thou hast thrilled with her touch, thou feelest still the Rhythm within thee unappeased and thou learnst that to appease it thou must go beyond. Call it love if thou wilt; what matters a name? I call it Tao.

The beauty of woman is only a vague reflection of the formless beauty of Tao. The emotion she awakens in thee, the desire to

127

blot thyself out in her beauty…believe me, it is nothing else than the rhythm of Tao, only thou knowest it not…. Seek not thy happiness in a woman. She is the revelation of Tao offering itself to thee, she is the purest form in Nature by which Tao manifests; she is the Force which awakens in thee the Rhythm of Tao—but by herself she is only a poor creature like thyself. And thou art for her the same revelation as she is for thee. It is the expression of Tao who has no limit nor form, and what they soul desires in the rapture which the vision of it causes thee, this strange and ineffable sentiment, is nought else than union with that Beauty and with the source of that Beauty—with Tao.

*Thy soul has lost its beloved Tao with whom it was formerly united and it desires reunion with the Beloved. An absolute reunion with Tao—is it not boundless Love? To be so absolutely one with the Beloved that thou art entirely hers and she entirely thine—a union so complete and so eternal that neither life nor death can ever separate thee, so peaceful and pure that Desire can no longer awaken in thee, because the supreme happiness is attained and there is only peace, peace sacred, calm, and luminous. For Tao is the Infinite of the soul, one, eternal, and all-pure.**

Love is a rapturous feeling one experiences when there is recognition of that formless beauty that rests within oneself and the ecstasy of self-realization.

The advice in this chapter issues a challenge that is, without question, life-altering. You may feel overwhelmed by it all, as I did when I first began. But these are goals, and by their very nature, aspirations are

---

* *Vijnanabhaurava or Divine Consciousness*, by Jaideva Singh

never within easy reach. Do not feel discouraged if you are out of shape, swigging booze, and about to sit down to a steak dinner. You will notice this chapter does not include a timetable. This is not a competition. There are no finish lines. As I did, you will try and fail and try again; but the important thing is that you never abandon your objectives or forget your goals; the remembrance of Lord Siva is all-important.

If you are resolved to become more refined spiritually, begin with the gross changes—give up meat, physical violence, sexual improprieties, and bad health habits; overcome addictions and eating disorders; get treatment for chronic depression and so on—then move to the subtle changes—speak nonviolently and, ultimately, take absolute control over the creator/protector/destroyer. Achieve a total purity of action. Overcoming bad habits is the first step in a long journey that can be slow but is inevitably thrilling. Nothing in my life has been as exciting or fulfilling as striving to adhere to Lakshmanjoo's teachings.

I seize every opportunity in each day to be brave, no matter what; to be nurturing, supportive, uplifting, and loving, especially to my family, even when I seem to be in the depths of failure, depression, or ruination. I exert my willpower not only to control my behavior and deeds but also to pilot my thoughts and mental dialogue. Every moment of the day brings opportunities to test my will power and strength. This is the practice of Karma Yoga. It is the most wonderful thing I have ever done—working toward self-control, living by a code of ethics, and seeing how powerful I can become. Instead of being a burden, ethical behavior becomes the ultimate game. And then, out of nowhere, by God's grace, comes compassion.

The fruit of this endeavor is for my own benefit, but it uplifts everybody, especially the ones I love. What material rewards—a fancy car, sexy secret lover, lavish rack-of-lamb dinner, wily business coup, or act of revenge against another—could possibly surpass developing the will power to find inner serenity, raise a beautiful child, enjoy a happy marriage, feel a genuine sense of unity with all God's creatures, and know and accept who I truly am? None of it comes close.

Practicing Shaivism does not mean that you have to change your life completely. Most of what you work on is subtle change in your behavior. Continue to participate in all the activities you enjoy, within the context of refinement and good action. Enjoy movies and television, go out to dinner, dance, whatever you like—these things are pleasurable and fun. Conquering nature is a subtle sort of thing. How we conduct ourselves, our speech, our gentleness—this is what is important. Many people think one must live an austere existence, becoming some sort of antisocial nut and renouncing everything to become one with God. This is not for Shaivites. The Shaivite embraces the world and at the same time is not affected by it.

Last but not least, I need to discuss the importance of developing positive thinking. The destroyer and protector fill your mind with negativity. They cast a frightening, gruesome picture on the screen of your conscious awareness. They make you picture the world in a way that is, at times, too much to handle. With practice you can learn to push these negative thoughts aside and fill your mind with more pleasant and uplifting mental dialogue. This mental dialogue in itself changed my life completely. Now that I know why I think the way I do, progress is easy.

Real change takes years, so do not be discouraged when you fail. My best advice is to never forget your goals; keep trying and eventually you will succeed. Developing strength of will and taking control requires tremendous courage and undying perseverance.

Chapter Sixteen

Lord Siva: A Journey of Self-Discovery

WHAT DOES IT FEEL LIKE TO HAVE ATTAINED THAT SUPREME STATE of being, to be Lord Siva fully realized while still residing in a body? Joy, incredible joy! To be God and know you are God; that experience is joy, a state of being that is unshakable, a feeling that is so overwhelming that nothing worldly can undermine it.

When you set out on this journey of self-realization, something wonderful begins to happen—joy starts to fill your heart. You can tell that progress is being made in this grand adventure by this joy that starts to fill your being.

For fools, on the other hand, everything is fleeting and transitory; nothing lasts. For them, everything has an end; sweet success, personal victories, love, the joy of sex, even life itself comes to an end. Fools are repeatedly shattered. Why and by whom? By God, of course, and for no other purpose except to get their attention. There is no other purpose for being here except to pursue self-realization, and it is none other than Lord Siva who is trying to turn our focus on Him. As a woman wants the love of a man or a man wants the love of a woman, so does God want the love of those who would discover who they are. It is this commitment and single-minded devotion to Him that is necessary to discover this incomprehensible joy. This joy is His joy and that is what this super-drama is all about. Those who do not understand or do not care are tormented and tortured.

In the final analysis, the limited individual and Lord Siva are one and the same, the worshipper and the worshipped also one, the disciple and the fully realized master the same. Both spectrums of this one Being exist simultaneously. But limited individuals have absolutely no understanding or comprehension of their other half. They are completely cut off from their unlimited state of being. Most people have no idea that anything else even exists. But it is Lord Siva, God almighty, that rests in the abode of the unlimited, and it is from this perspective that this incredible game is orchestrated. This is a game where Lord Siva loses Himself in the manifest world and it is also Lord Siva who helps Himself rediscover His own Self again. Remember, Lord Siva exists simultaneously as the supreme "I" and as the lost soul in humanity. He is both. How fantastic to be able to do so.

God reigns supreme over the events that take place in this worldly existence. Unfortunately, most humans have absolutely no idea of their relationship to the divine; they believe they are free agents caught up in a drama that is totally their own. This, however, is absurd. It is Lord Siva who punishes, only to elevate. It is God who strikes fear and chronic anxiety into the hearts of those who are not focused on Him, only to get their attention. There is always a reason things turn out the way they do, and whatever that may be, it always rests with the divine.

Most people start out with unbridled enthusiasm for life, love, passion, marriage, children, money—all the things we hold so dear to our heart. Invariably, one way or the other, time and time again it is all smashed. Like a clod of dirt, our life crumbles right before our eyes. While holding it in the palm of our hand, our dreams of happiness-ever-after turn to dust. There is good reason our heart is so heavy and we suffer from one nervous breakdown after another, why depression always seems to be lurking just this side of the next disaster on the way. Our frustration is so great that we are perpetually on the verge of exploding. No one has the faintest idea as to the solution to life's misery. People will do almost anything to escape from their pain and suffering.

To be God and not know that you are God is the ultimate frustration, because even in the furthest recesses of the mind of the most ignorant, there is a trace of remembrance—and thus a frustration; there is no rest or peace of mind in this existence for anybody. But the meaning of life is hidden; this trace of remembrance is just that, a trace and nothing more. Fools have no idea who God is and why life turns out the way it does. Time and again, Lord Siva tries to get their attention, to no avail. How very difficult it is to get some to play the game.

When people begin to understand, they start to let go of their pain and suffering. They can see with newfound clarity what is happening and, for the first time in their life, experience a change of heart.

Only when Lord Siva becomes the central figure in our life can this begin to occur. Lord Siva is the central theme in our life whether we know it or not, and when this is discovered, the adventure begins. It is at this point that pain and suffering begin to melt away.

Lord Siva is there every second of the day, totally involved in everything we do. The whys and wherefores of life reside only with Him. We can blame anybody we want for each little predicament, but this is absurd. We can blame our spouse for our misery, for not understanding; we can blame our parents for the way we turned out, unhappy and chronically depressed; we can blame our boss for the way he or she treats us. But if we must blame somebody, blame God. He is responsible for everything. Everything rises out of and sinks back into His consciousness; He is all that manifests.

Those who complain of the injustice in this world are whining fools. Some people will never get better, because their bitterness cuts too deep and the role of the victim is too ingrained in their being. On the other hand, this knowledge alone should be enough for a person to see the magic in this great wisdom and allow for a new beginning, to start healing old wounds and building a new life. After all, it was God all along who has been playing with you. All He wants is you! The individual characters you hold responsible for your predicament are themselves Lord Siva. How could you take this personally? All He wants is your attention. Instead of existing in a constant state of shock and disbelief as to the mess you find yourself in, from this point forward it would be more appropriate to ask *Why is this happening to me? What am I doing wrong? What is God trying to tell me?*

Practically speaking, life can become a lot less complicated and certainly simpler to understand under this philosophy. This philosophy takes the sting out of life and gives its practitioner great hope. The wise take total refuge in Lord Siva. He is That who gives all and takes all, so why retreat to any other corner but His?

This does not mean that you should not have an operation if it is needed, or refuse to take antibiotics for some sort of infectious disease.

This would be stupid. Ultimately, though, God will oversee the outcome of each and every circumstance of your life.

Therefore, the wise put themselves at His feet with no expectations whatsoever. As these devotees to Lord Siva become ever more steadfast in their faith, they worry less about what the future has in store. They do the best they can at whatever is required as participating inhabitants of this world and leave the rest to God. Only fools worry themselves sick over things they cannot control. I should know—I was the biggest of fools. Day and night, fools fret themselves into a state of oblivion, and for what? For nothing. What is going to be is out of our hands, so why worry? The strength of our faith is directly proportional to our level of anxiety—or, in this case, the lack of it. Whether good or bad, it is all Lord Siva's play, so why not relax and enjoy?

Why should I be filled with disappointment when things do not turn out the way I wish? Now I try to take the good and the bad with a grain of salt. When plans fall apart or somebody breaks a promise or a commitment, I relax and see the drama in it, not the disappointment. There is no reason for me to go up and down anymore. Up and down, disappointment and elation; this seesaw of opposites is for fools. It is Lord Siva who is making all these last-minute changes in my life anyway, so where is the room for anger or disbelief? Although limited beings cannot understand why things turn out the way they do, their faith in the unlimited should be all that is necessary. It is from this vantage point, and only from this vantage point, that you can truly develop peace of mind. This is the seed of true joy.

There is no reason to fret over the details that unravel in our life. This is a challenge that requires constant remembrance. Detachment is the key, and enjoyment—even amusement. The wise simply enjoy the drama that unfolds before them; who cares about the results? It is God's drama, not ours. But this takes practice. This comes with time. It is a challenge. This is how one gives up the world. On the other hand, the fool is either in seventh heaven or feeling destroyed, depending on what is happening. Fools believe this is their drama, that they are the author of what is happening.

Equally amusing is the fools' constant chatter as they proclaim to anyone who will listen a new course of action for their life that collapses before their words have hardly left their mouth. "I am going to do this," "I am going to do that," "I'll never do that again." Fools' words mean next to nothing. There is no strength in them. What they say they are going to do and what actually happens to them are two different things. Guess who is responsible for this. The wiser someone gets, the less someone says. How very playful is this incredible Being.

From this point forward, life does not have to be filled with disappointment, heartache, and unhappiness. Life should be exciting, with an ever-increasing joy that fills the heart. There is no reason to take life so seriously anymore. But this takes faith, total surrender to Lord Siva: "Oh dear and mighty God, I am totally yours, I am putting myself in your hands, do with me as you will." "Please protect me and guide me in my journey unto thee." This takes great humility. It is the admission of knowing nothing but wanting to know everything, the admission of total vulnerability but wanting to become immutable and eternal. It is the admission of being almost totally powerless but wanting to be God. This is the beginning of a pact, a covenant; the development of a relationship that is like no other. In the beginning, this relationship with Lord Siva is like the imaginary play of a child. After some time it becomes ever more real in your mind as your life begins to change. It is a relationship in which God becomes the witness of our actions, the protector and the helper. It is at this point that our work truly begins. To make that transition from the fool to self-realization requires effort.

The spiritual seeker can no longer add to the pain and suffering of the world. In this state of limitation, Lord Siva forgets that everything that surrounds Him is an expansion of His own self. He does not know that when He looks into the eyes of another it is Himself staring back. So, this person, the spiritual aspirant, must practice being kind, understanding, and uplifting, never condescending or cruel. This person must learn to become nonviolent in every aspect of its meaning. Spiritual aspirants must keep in the back of their mind at all times that everything and everyone is divine and therefore should be treated with respect, even reverence; that all things are an expansion of Lord Siva (of their own self).

At this point you must ask yourself, *What kind of a person am I? How do I treat my family, friends, coworkers, and fellow human beings?* Fools always picture themselves in a favorable light with clear justification for all of their actions. I speak from experience; no one was more self-righteous than I was. Fools have absolutely no self-awareness at any level and therefore cannot change. Unlike the fool, those who begin to develop awareness start to see how their actions affect the world around them. Then and only then can change begin to take place.

Awareness is the key in this adventure from the beginning to its end. It is awareness that brings the aspirant to the doorstep of the divine. At first this awareness is applied to the most gross physical aspects of our limited reality, our own personal behavior. This requires great awareness. After some time, this awareness is applied to a more subtle reality, the reality of the Unlimited.

What an incredible adventure! Nothing is more exciting. All else pales in comparison to this journey of self-discovery. When God truly gets the attention of His devotee, then everything changes. Lord Siva ignites that trace of remembrance that rests in our mind and then clears the way. It is His ocean of compassion that floods over us in the form of Grace. Truly does He love those who are focused on Him.

God loves everyone, it is true. But what can He do if the individual does not love Him? Can there be a relationship between a man and a woman if one is totally disinterested in the other or if one of the parties involved does not even know that the other party exists? Can there be a relationship if one is perpetually in a state of anger and rage, disrespectful, and totally unrefined in every way? Even when Lord Siva "rattles their cage," shatters their life, throws them into ruination, inflicts them with disease, chronic anxiety, and depression, most never figure it out. Some, for a brief moment, turn their attention toward Him, only to forget again as soon as their life improves. For most, however, it is absolutely impossible to comprehend that this worldly existence is one divine superdrama with no other agenda except self-discovery. This is why God filled the world with fools, to make this game interesting.

Bringing ourselves under control takes considerable awareness and personal power. Ultimately, it is strength of will combined with this awareness that determines success. This is no ordinary adventure but an extraordinary challenge. What we are confronting is nature, our own nature. The body, mind, and emotions have their own preset agenda that is set in the field of opposites. Nature herself is composed of opposites. Coagulated consciousness, that which takes on shape and form and operates in the realm of time, is built out of opposites and therefore becomes the nature of our own limited being. For humans this equates to love and hate. As a creator/destroyer, we are filled with an equal amount of love and hate and unleash these powerful opposites on the world. To bring ourselves under control is to go against the grain of nature—no easy task.

This is not an easy game to play, especially in the beginning. To be something other than the fool takes nothing short of a miracle; to become aware, controlled, and willful—a very tall order. It can be done, and there is great joy for those who can do it.

As our strength increases, so does our relationship with the divine. It becomes a love where each is devoted to the other. Limited individual beings cannot progress on their own, nor, without this attention and devotion, can the unlimited give them what they need. Only together, each committed to the other, does this union of the limited with the unlimited occur. This is a grand adventure!

Chapter Seventeen

Lakshmanjoo and
Hope for the Future

I am Bhairava* and the entire world is my offshoot.

Siva is the only great God and all others are his manifestations.

God is the inner being; the entire world is his external being.

THOSE THREE STATEMENTS SUM UP THE ENLIGHTENED MIND OF THIS great Being, elucidate monism, and the essence of Kashmir Shaivism.

Today the radiance of this flame [the teachings of Kashmir Shaivism] is seen in a small but beautiful Ashram, situated at the

---

* Bhairava is the aspect of Lord Siva that destroys the individual ego in the spiritual aspirant; Grace is the revealing aspect of Lord Siva.

*foot of a mountain, not many miles distant from the historic Harwan forest, and only a few furlongs from the famous Mughal garden, Nishat. While Nature has bestowed picturesqueness on the Ashram, its peace and harmony really radiate from its maintainer, Rajanaka Lakshman [Swami Ishvar Svarup Ji] popularly called Lakshman Joo. He follows the Masters [Somananda, Utpala, Abhinavagupta]. Scholars and students, coming from all the corners of the country and from foreign lands, too, find in His exposition of Shaivism the tone and depth of Abhinavagupta, and the sweetness and light of Utpala; and, for hundreds of devotees of different faiths, He is a living image of God—this Philosopher and sixty-three-year-old Yogi and Brahmachari. He shines like a steady flame of love and peace; He brings rest to the most restless of things, the human mind. It is only when you meet Him that you feel Him, and when you feel Him you begin to love Him and this love becomes purer and more and yet more irresistible as days pass, and a time comes when you realize that in Him you have discovered your best friend and a sympathizer; a time comes, sooner then you would expect, when you discover an alluring sweetness of a childlike innocence behind the gravity of His philosophic exterior. Like a supremely beautiful thing, a sunset lingering on a snow peak, a full-blown lotus bewitched by its image on the bluish waters of a calm lake, a note of music struck by a master musician in his most inspired moment, the Swami sinks into your mind, sure to reappear to bring you peace and hope in the darkest moment of your life as a rainbow emerging on a stormy sky. His silence speaks; it speaks of the reality of the Spirit; it speaks of the gateway to God, of the path that leads to real liberation.**

---

* Professor T. N. Bhan, *The Malini,* a publication of the Ishwar Ashram Trust, Ishber (Nishat), Srinagar, Kashmir. *The Malini,* a regularly published booklet, is a combination of Lakshmanjoo's teachings and inspirational insights by his Kashmiri devotees.

As fate would have it, I found much more than I ever anticipated on my journey to self-discovery. Lakshmanjoo changed my life forever. The knowledge and wisdom that he so graciously bestowed upon me dramatically altered my outlook on everything, especially with regard to how I see myself. After spending much of my life feeling unworthy and flawed, I awoke to the realization that I had been a divine creature waiting to be roused from unconscious slumber.

Lakshmanjoo heightened my senses in a way that is difficult to describe. A masterful teacher, he made God real and tangible for me. My appreciation for the Almighty is becoming greater each day. I have become aware that this whole existence is God's drama, and everything going on around me—the small talk, the idle chatter, the emotions—is an extension of something people rarely, if ever, get a glimpse of or even know exists.

Instead of existing in a hostile world where nothing makes sense, I now live in an environment where I know what is happening. Because of my insights, my marriage is wonderful, and my wife can do no wrong. I understand her; she understands me. We are raising a special child filled with self-esteem and pride. I know the nature of our daughter's heart and how to work with it. How utterly fantastic! Just appreciating and knowing what is going on has changed everything.

I have learned that everything in life is filled with contradiction, and I know now that I must control these inconsistencies in myself in order to be powerful. Meeting this inner psyche head-on and becoming only good are the ultimate challenges. They mean a day-to-day bout between a new part of myself—an awareness and appreciation that only a human could have—pitted against something bigger than life itself.

The absolute measure of a person in this game is the strength of his or her will and level of conscious awareness. Practicing medicine, making complex financial decisions, solving intricate mathematical equations, and building new technologies for an easier and more comfortable lifestyle mean nothing in comparison. Their compensations are limited. Compassion, understanding, and purity of character offer infinite rewards and take practice. To be the creator/protector/destroyer and become this kind of person is the challenge. I am prepared to fail and when I do, I just start over again. When I fail, I do not feel guilty or ashamed, just determined to succeed. These methods may be mastered within a relatively short period of time, or it may take ten or fifteen years to get going. It does not matter.

Each moment of the day brings a new challenge. Your whole life becomes a testing ground for this marvelous undertaking. The process is a self-promoting, self-illuminating, self-propelling journey. The passage is part of the excitement and joy. What Kashmir Shaivism offers is not didactic, philosophical rhetoric. What I am describing is not all or nothing. Remembrance and practice are the key. Kashmir Shaivism is scientific. You can prove it to yourself.

For those who consider themselves twentieth-century thinkers, sophisticates, whose religion is science—fine; after all, God is the ultimate science. This physical reality and the science that explains it is the study of the grossest, outermost aspect of this divine being. God is this physical reality plus the subtleties that rest behind it. The sciences of anatomy, physiology, mathematics, physics, supernova explosions, and the death of stars is the study of a single entity: God. From the ridiculous theories of ignorant fools to the supreme understanding of the blessed ones, it pours outward from a single source. No matter what it appears to be on the surface, there is just one thing that is everything.

This game has a one-person team, and the sole member is you. What I suggest is that you discover your own self, as I have. Look behind the scenes. Be aware of what you are doing, what you are thinking and saying, and how you behave. I hardly ever take my awareness off my own state of being these days; but when I do, I sink. Try to see how you interact with the world, people, situations, friends, and family. What you think and your opinions originate with the creator, protector, or destroyer. Your judgments on your next-door neighbor, Congress, and the president ride through your consciousness and are altered by the passion of your inner beings.

I try to be kind and understanding even to those who are gross, crass, and destructive. Seeing the divinity in everyone—even though they are, on the surface, despicable and plotting my seduction or destruction—is the ultimate challenge. I know by now that I cannot expect anything true and straight from others. Expectations only bring frustration and disappointment.

If we truly develop control over our sexual and violent natures by developing real mental and physical character with purity of body, mind, speech, we will have no reason to look over our shoulder for retribution for past deeds. The world will leave us alone and allow us to rest. Otherwise we become fair game for the Player that creates its actors, then swallows them whole, that gives with one hand and smashes with the other, that whispers "I love you" into our ear and simultaneously tears out our heart. This is how many parents treat each other and their children.

As I developed skills in keeping with Lakshmanjoo's teachings, pain and suffering dropped away. Meanness, cruelty, and violence are kept at bay. Those who can integrate this great knowledge into the daily activity of their lives will be protected by the grace of God. It is difficult to understand at first, but protection comes from within, not from outside forces. You protect yourself, by yourself, with your own self. You need to remember who you are. You have imposed this on yourself and made your own rules.

The wiser we become, the more cognizant we will be of how our personal actions affect our lives. We are not isolated beings or free spirits. Quite the contrary. Our own personal life is a relationship with Lord Siva. We are immersed in His presence; as in any relationship, how we treat Him determines how He treats us.

By the grace of God in Its highest form and incarnated in Lakshmanjoo, the Almighty has brought to a close an era of ignorance and darkness for humanity.

O, dear God, I bow to Thee for making this so!

Chapter Eighteen

Putting It All Together

YOU HAVE COME A LONG WAY. I HOPE THIS JOURNEY OF SELF-DISCOVery has been as exciting for you as it has been for me. But the work is yet to begin. The goal is to implement this philosophy into your daily living so that it empowers your existence in the here and now and ultimately prepares you to rise. Although most people must work for a living and thus expend a great deal of effort in simply surviving, those who have enough energy left over to incorporate these ideas into their daily living will no longer have to suffer from the tragedy of life that befalls the limited being. This final chapter outlines the ideas that remain foremost in my mind.

What tremendous power rests in what we call Consciousness. Consciousness is Divine. That Being who possesses it is the Eternal One. That is what He is, Consciousness. This Consciousness is undividable, immutable, unchangeable—it just is. It is pure awareness. What is it aware of? It is aware of nothing other than Its own self. Because this Divine Consciousness has the power to take on shape and form, it becomes aware. The subject and the object, the knower and the known, the perceiver and that which is perceived, are all one. In other words, Consciousness is either the perceiving awareness or the object of perception. This is the power of Consciousness.

Therefore there is just one thing, Divine Consciousness, the Eternal One, Lord Siva. In this divine drama, the Eternal Being takes on a multitude of shapes and forms as it pleases Him. As described in Chapter Five, this process of manifestation, or the congealment of consciousness, occurs by the process contained within the thirty-six tattvas, the downward ladder by which Lord Siva descends into this world—a progressive constriction of His nature. He descends and ascends by this same ladder.

As limited beings toward the bottom of this ladder (at least we are not dirt or a piece of rock), our awareness now is such that our surrounding world appears separate from our own self. We cannot experience the wholeness contained within the unity of consciousness, nor can we feel its power. Quite a predicament considering that we are God.

Now that we are here, we have to do something about it. But first, a little more explanation. As limited beings, we do three things: We take in the outside world with our senses; we think about this world and the objects contained within it; and we act upon the world.

Ultimately, to ascend, we must give up our fascination with this manifest world. Of course, until now there was no reason to even consider such a thing. Why should we? Who could deny our fanatical preoccupation with this existence? We are here, this is our life, we are up to our neck in it. "I need this," "I need that," "I hate this," "I love that"—there is an unbroken chain of attachment to this existence.

148

To rise, we must give up this world and all the fascinating things that hold us to it. We cannot ascend or rise if we cannot let go. Dying does nothing; we just start over with another body; that is, we are born again. But there has to be a starting point, something more tangible for the beginning student, something more pertinent to the here and now. The thought of giving up this world is too much for most. Help is what everyone needs; help in incorporating this philosophy into our daily living such that we start on this journey, and because of this, improve the quality of our existence. To do this, the student of Kashmir Shaivism must see the overall picture of divinity and then work on love and hate, to begin to bring these powerful forces under control. This is the first step in the process of letting go of this world, with tremendous practical benefit. Of course, a little detachment would not hurt either. Now that you know who is in charge, try to relax a little. Do not be so affected by all the little details of your life. This is where joy begins.

Foremost on my mind:

To realize who I am; to contemplate this. To realize that my life is the playing field of a game that I myself have created. To realize that this whole existence is an expansion of my own self, that all the characters contained within this existence are an extension of me. To remember that when I look into another's eyes, it is my own self staring back. This is the play of Consciousness. This is remembrance, my own play. Over time, this concept is growing in my mind, forming a bridge between the finite and the infinite.

To realize that everyone is Lord Siva. I am Lord Siva, my wife is Lord Siva, my child is Lord Siva, my friends and enemies are Lord Siva, my pets are Lord Siva. When I am sitting at the dinner table with my family or watching television in the evening with them, I know who I am in the presence of; it is God sitting across the table from me—they are He!

To realize that when I am interacting with others, I am really interacting with Lord Siva. To remind myself constantly that part of the trick is to comprehend how all-encompassing this philosophy is as it applies to my daily life. How easily I forget. If all this is God's play, then certainly whatever I do is playing with God. If everyone is in fact Lord Siva, then everything I do is direct interaction with Him. The person to whom I am talking, responding, or giving, or the one I am receiving from in my daily routine, is none other than Lord Siva. If I request something from a friend, I am really making that request of God. If I receive something from another, I am receiving it from God. Anything that comes my way or goes away is God's doing. This is how I try to think.

To serve other people is to serve God. What a wonderful outlook. It has changed my heart completely. That animosity, that chip on my shoulder, those feelings of futility about this existence are starting to melt away. How tragic not to know. As I talk to someone, as I stare out into a crowd, as I interact with my wife or child, I see them all as Lord Siva.

To learn to adore everything. As every single thing that happens is part of God's divine drama, then bad news should be adored as well as good news. It is hard to comprehend that whatever is going on is God's drama, that He Himself is responsible for all the twists and turns that befall me in my journey in life. Remembrance is the key. It is hard to remember that this is His journey, not mine. But He and I are one and the same—this is my trick. Rather than be judgmental, positive or negative, up or down, depending on what is going on, I stand back and think, "This is all His doing" and remain in awe. Whether getting fired or getting promoted, whether winning or losing, whether succeeding or failing, it is all God's play. It is a game; the challenge for me now is to see it as such: to be involved in this game but unaffected by its outcome; to remain the same whether winning or losing; in adoration and awe, to see all action in this world as Lord Siva's.

To understand that, under the circumstances, there is nothing to worry about. All I can do is the best I can, and whatever happens after that is out of my hands. What else can I do?

To understand that there is no meaning in worldly success; there is no meaning in titles and prestigious awards, wealth, fame, or fortune. There is nothing wrong with any of these things, but in themselves, they are nothing—less than the dust on my shoe. What seemed so valuable to me is simply fool's gold and nothing more—worthless.

Detachment comes from the way I think, not from austerity. Moving to the end of the road in Alaska to escape this world accomplishes nothing. The measure of my success is to become detached from or unaffected by this world while standing squarely in the middle of it; neither loving nor hating, caring less about the fruit of success or the throes of failure; standing steady no matter what is happening. Truly has my heart begun to fill with joy, after a bleakness I could barely stand. Keeping the bigger picture in the back of my mind at all times and behaving ethically has changed everything for me. For the first time, I am truly becoming happy and content. "Just be it" keeps sounding in my mind.

To surrender myself completely to Lord Siva; to seek refuge in no other corner. Every day, every hour, every minute, every second of my existence is by Lord Siva's grace, such that I might discover Him within my own being.

To ask for forgiveness for all of the horrible things that I have done; for all those whom I have hurt.

To remember, above all else, that I am the creator/protector/destroyer. This is who I am. My first step is to bring these forces under control, to be only good and uplifting, and, above all else, to develop purity of body, mind, and speech—purity of action.

I do have a will and a choice. By God's grace, I am making progress. I thank Him for this greatest of all adventures.

To know that awareness is the key in this endeavor. How could I bring the creator/protector/destroyer under control unless I am aware of what I am doing as each moment of the day passes? I must constantly be aware of what I am about to say, what I am about to do, and how I am about to behave, including the tone of voice that is on the verge of leaving my mouth and lips. Otherwise I will remain a fool in a fool's drama, building up my life with one hand and smashing it with the other. By God's grace, every day is a new challenge. Now my strength can be measured by the strength of my awareness and the strength of my will, to bring myself under total control where no anger or violence leaks from my being.

To become physically and mentally fit is a must. I have given up bad habits such as smoking, alcohol, and recreational drugs. I have quit eating meat. I am striving for refinement in every aspect of my life.

To gain courage. What I lacked most was courage, and now, by God's grace, it is growing by leaps and bounds. Each day I feel as if I am coming closer to Lord Siva—but still, to my dismay, there are times when I forget everything; I forget who I am and sink to the bottom. In the confusion of the moment, I forget, and my strength leaves. It is only when I remember Him that my strength and awareness return.

I give myself to You, Lord Siva, to do with as you please. I am Yours.
Om Namah Shivaya
(Om! To Siva I bow)

Additional Reading

Bailley, Constantina Rhodes. *Shaiva Devotional Songs of Kashmir.* Albany, NY: State University of New York Press, 1987.

Dyczkowski, Mark. *The Doctrine of Vibration.* Albany, NY: State University of New York Press, 1989.

Hughes, John. *Self-Realization in Kashmir Shaivism: The Oral Teachings of Swami Lakshmanjoo.* Albany, NY: State University of New York Press, 1994. (Can be purchased directly from John Hughes at 10925 Stever Street, Culver City, CA 90230.)
For those interested in learning more about Kashmir Shaivism and Swami Lakshmanjoo, this new book by John Hughes is a must. Kashmir Shaivism, The Secret Supreme *by Swami Lakshmanjoo is also available from John Hughes.*

Ksemaraja. *The Doctrine of Recognition.* Translation by Jaideva Singh. Albany, NY: State University of New York Press, 1990.

Lakshmanjoo, Swami. *Kashmir Shaivism: The Secret Supreme.* Kashmir, India: Universal Shaiva Trust, 1985. (Republished by SUNY Press, 1988.)
Recently republished in its entirety in John Hughes' book (see above).

_____. *Lectures on Practice and Discipline in Kashmir Shaivism.* Kashmir, India: Universal Shaiva Trust, 1982.

Singh, Jaideva. *Abhinavagupta.* Albany, NY: State University of New York Press, 1989.

_____. *Siva Sutras—The Yoga of Supreme Identity.* New Delhi, India: Motilal Banarsidas Publishers, 1990.

The Malini
2-Mohinder Nagar, Canal Road
Jammu TAWI 180002, India.
Produced by Ishwar Ashram Trust, this monthly publication offers some of the teachings of Swami Lakshmanjoo plus personal accounts and insights of His Indian devotees.

Index

Stay in Touch. . .

Llewellyn publishes hundreds of books on your favorite subjects!
On the following pages you will find listed some books now available on related subjects. Your local bookstore stocks most of these and will stock new Llewellyn titles as they become available. We urge your patronage.

Order by Phone

Call toll-free within the U.S. and Canada, **1–800–THE MOON**. In Minnesota call **(612) 291–1970**. We accept Visa, MasterCard, and American Express.

Order by Mail

Send the full price of your order (MN residents add 7% sales tax) in U.S. funds to:
> **Llewellyn Worldwide**
> **P.O. Box 64383, Dept. K522–3**
> **St. Paul, MN 55164–0383, U.S.A.**

Postage and Handling

◆ $4.00 for orders $15.00 and under
◆ $5.00 for orders over $15.00
◆ No charge for orders over $100.00

We ship UPS in the continental United States. We cannot ship to P.O. boxes. Orders shipped to Alaska, Hawaii, Canada, Mexico, and Puerto Rico will be sent first-class mail.

International orders: Airmail—add freight equal to price of each book to the total price of order, plus $5.00 for each non-book item (audiotapes, etc.). Surface mail—add $1.00 per item.

Allow 4–6 weeks delivery on all orders. Postage and handling rates subject to change.

Group Discounts

We offer a 20% quantity discount to group leaders or agents. You must order a minimum of 5 copies of the same book to get our special quantity price.

Free Catalog

Get a free copy of our color catalog, *New Worlds of Mind and Spirit.* Subscribe for just $10.00 in the United States and Canada ($20.00 overseas, first-class mail). Many bookstores carry *New Worlds*—ask for it!

A CHAKRA & KUNDALINI WORKBOOK
Psycho-Spiritual Techniques for Health,
Rejuvenation, Psychic Powers &
Spiritual Realization
Dr. Jonn Mumford
(Swami Anandakapila Saraswati)

Spend just a few minutes each day on the remarkable psycho-physiological techniques in this book and you will quickly build a solid experience of drugless inner relaxation that will lead towards better health, a longer life, and greater control over your personal destiny. Furthermore, you will lay a firm foundation for the subsequent chapters leading to the attainment of super-normal powers (i.e., photographic memory, self-anesthesia, and mental calculations), and ultimate transcendence. Learn techniques to use for burn-out, mild to moderate depression, insomnia, anxiety attacks, and reduction of mild to moderate hypertension. Experience sex for consciousness expansion, ESP development, and positive thinking. In addition, the author has added a simple outline of a 12-week practice schedule referenced to the first nine chapters.

A Chakra & Kundalini Workbook is one of the clearest, most approachable books on Yoga there is. Tailored for the Western mind, this is a practical system of personal training suited for anyone in today's active and complex world.

1-56718-473-1, 296 pp., 7 x 10, illus., color plates, softcover $17.95

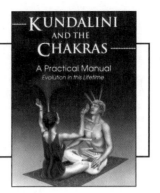

KUNDALINI AND THE CHAKRAS
A Practical Manual—
Evolution in this Lifetime
Genevieve Paulson

The mysteries of Kundalini revealed! We all possess the powerful evolutionary force of Kundalini that can open us to genius states, psychic powers, and cosmic consciousness. As the energies of the Aquarian Age intensify, more and more people are experiencing the "big release" spontaneously but have been ill-equipped to channel its force in a productive manner. This book shows you how to release Kundalini gradually and safely, and is your guide to sating the strange, new appetites that result when life-in-process "blows open" your body's many energy centers.

The section on chakras brings new understanding to these "dials" on our life machine (body). It is the most comprehensive information available for cleansing and developing the chakras and their energies. Read *Kundalini and the Chakras* and prepare to make a quantum leap in your spiritual growth!

0-87542-592-5, 224 pp,. 6 x 9, illus., color plates, softcover $14.95

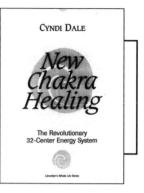

CYNDI DALE

New Chakra Healing

The Revolutionary
32-Center Energy System

Llewellyn's Whole Life Series

NEW CHAKRA HEALING
The Revolutionary 32-Center Energy System
Cyndi Dale

Break through the barriers that keep you from your true purpose with *New Chakra Healing*. This manual presents never-before-published information that makes a quantum leap in the current knowledge of the human energy centers, fields, and principles that govern the connection between the physical and spiritual realms.

By working with your full energy body, you can heal all resistance to living a successful life. The traditional seven-chakra system was just the beginning of our understanding of the holistic human. Now Cyndi Dale's research uncovers a total of 32 energy centers: 12 physically oriented chakras, and 20 energy points that exist in the spiritual plane. She also discusses auras, rays, kundalini, mana energy, karma, dharma, and cords (energetic connections between people that serve as relationship contracts). In addition, she extends chakra work to include the back of the body as well as the front, with detailed explanations on how these energy systems tie into the spine. Each chapter takes the reader on a journey through the various systems, incorporating personal experiences, practical exercises, and guided meditation.

1-56718-200-3, 288 pp., 7 x 10, illus., softcover   **$17.95**

To order, call 1-800-THE-MOON
All prices subject to change without notice

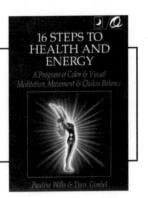

16 Steps to Health and Energy
A Program of Color & Visual Meditation,
Movement & Chakra Balance
Pauline Wills & Theo. Gimble

Before an illness reaches your physical body, it has already been in your auric body for days, weeks, even months. By the time you feel sick, something in your life has been out of balance for a while. But why wait to get sick to get healthy? Follow the step-by-step techniques in *16 Steps to Health and Energy,* and you will open up the energy circuits of your subtle body so you are better able to stay balanced and vital in our highly toxic and stressful world.

Our subtle anatomy includes the "energy" body of 7 chakras that radiate the seven colors of the spectrum. Each chakra responds well to a particular combination of yoga postures and color visualizations, all of which are provided in this book.

At the end of the book is a series of 16 "workshops" that help you to travel through progressive stages of consciousness expansion and self-transformation. Each session deals with a particular color and all of its associated meditations, visualizations, and yoga postures. Here is a truly holistic route to health at all levels! Includes 16 color plates!

0-87542-871-1, 224 pp., 6 x 9, illus., softcover   **$12.95**